The Pocket Mentor for Careers in VFX

Want to progress your career as a CG artist? Then this is the book for you. This book provides all the essential information and guidance you need to understand the industry, get your foot on the ladder, and further your career.

This book looks at a wide range of job roles within the VFX pipeline, such as modeler, surfacing artist, lighting artist, FX artist, rigger, animator, and compositor. It explains the most common day-to-day tasks performed within the role, the tools used, and how to learn them. It provides the essential information needed to progress from any of these positions to a lead role and eventually CG supervisor.

Packed with real-world insights, this book features interviews with experienced VFX professionals working in different disciplines, offering valuable career advice and a behind-the-scenes look at their journeys.

This book will be useful to those looking to enter the industry as well as those already working within it and that are looking to further advance their career.

David Ferreira is CG Supervisor at Accenture Song VFX.

The Pocket Mentors for Games Careers Series

The Pocket Mentors for Games Careers provide the essential information and guidance needed to get and keep a job in the modern games industry. They explain in simple, clear language exactly what a beginner needs to know about education requirements, finding job opportunities, applying for roles, and acing studio interviews. Readers will learn how to navigate studio hierarchies, transfer roles and companies, work overseas, and develop their skills.

The Pocket Mentor for Video Game Writers
Anna Megill

The Pocket Mentor for Video Game Testing
Harún Ali

The Pocket Mentor for Game Community Management
Carolin Wendt

The Pocket Mentor for Animators
Hollie Newsham

The Pocket Mentor for Game Audio
Greg Lester and Jonny Sands

The Pocket Mentor for Video Game UX UI
Simon Brewer

The Pocket Mentor for Game Production
Doug Pennant

The Pocket Mentor for Careers in VFX
David Ferreira

For more information about this series, please visit: https://www.routledge.com/The-Pocket-Mentors-for-Games-Careers/book-series/PMGC

The Pocket Mentor for Careers in VFX

David Ferreira

CRC Press
Taylor & Francis Group
Boca Raton London New York

CRC Press is an imprint of the
Taylor & Francis Group, an **informa** business

Designed cover image: David Ferreira

First edition published 2026
by CRC Press
2385 NW Executive Center Drive, Suite 320, Boca Raton FL 33431

and by CRC Press
4 Park Square, Milton Park, Abingdon, Oxon, OX14 4RN

CRC Press is an imprint of Taylor & Francis Group, LLC

© 2026 David Ferreira

ISBN: 9781032799193 (hbk)
ISBN: 9781032795799 (pbk)
ISBN: 9781003494485 (ebk)

DOI: 10.1201/9781003494485

Typeset in Times
by codeMantra

Contents

Introduction

1

ABOUT THE AUTHOR HAVING NO IDEA WHAT HE WANTED TO DO

FIGURE 1.1 Kimera—personal project depicting a CG student.

I was raised in a small fishing village called Nazaré in Portugal, long before it became known worldwide for its gigantic waves. I grew up with the label of a very bright student and a promising future, so during the final years of high school, when having to make decisions about how and where to continue my education, I felt I had a lot of options but at the same time very little certainty. I really valued and cultivated, to the best of my abilities, the concept of

DOI: 10.1201/9781003494485-1   1

Homo Universalis. My curiosity had no boundaries, so it was really hard for me to pick a single area of knowledge. Eventually decided to go for a degree in Biology, hoping to be able to have close contact with animals and maybe help save part of our beaten-down planet.

At the university, I found myself quickly losing interest in the classes and dedicating more time to other fields and a lot of bohemia. When I finished my degree with a low score, I had nothing lined up in terms of work or an internship. There was also clearly not enough passion left in me to chase anything.

At that point in my life, money was a real concern and becoming more and more a factor to take into account on my decisions in regard to my professional future. Working part time for about a year, reflecting on what I would really like to do that would have good financial prospects, I ended up preparing myself for the admission exams in a completely different area—I decided I wanted to study Architecture. So, I tapped into that bright student in me once again and managed to get into the main Architecture University in Lisbon.

The course was going well but was very expensive in terms of all the materials you need to buy to build your models, draw,…, which meant I needed to work part time as well or find some other source of income. And here enters 3D Studio Max to change everything.

In one of my classes, I believe it was called Digital Drawing, we were introduced to 3D Studio Max on a very basic level for the purpose of visualizing our projects in 3D. I was immediately fascinated by it. One of the things that drove me toward Architecture was the combination of drawing, geometry, and math. 3D Studio Max seemed to be the embodiment of that and a much cheaper solution to recreating my projects without the whole expense of actual materials to build it. Around the same time a close friend of mine (who took a degree in Arts and then got into a limited edition and limited access intensive course of Animation in 3D) was making good money working for a company that was recreating Macau in 3D using low poly models done in 3D Studio Max and textured with Photoshop all based on photos provided by the company. This was an ambitious project and somewhat pioneer at the time. I thought I had enough skills to do it as well, so I asked my friend to introduce me, and after a small test, I got hired.

This was the absolute game changer.

A very well-paid job with no strict hours, so totally compatible with my studies, and something that I realized I could easily do for hours in a row without even noticing the time pass by. I became the company's top performer and suddenly had a financial freedom I hadn't experienced before. I had found my calling and decided to go all in.

I dropped my Architecture degree at the end of the 3rd year, invested in a better computer, and dedicated myself to learning 3D for Architecture Visualization on my own. The goal was to have the best portfolio I could make in 3 months and start sending it along with my CV to the main ArchViz studios in Lisbon.

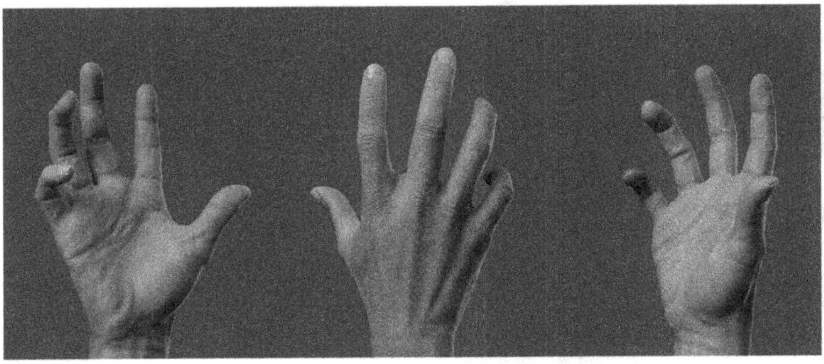

FIGURE 1.2   Sculpting and texturing my own hand.

It paid off.

Got a position at Arqui300 as a junior 3D artist and that still feels like the official beginning of my career in the world of 3D back in 2008. At Arqui300, I was exposed to people with much more knowledge and experience than I had. I soaked it all and soon it wasn't enough to satisfy my curiosity, my will to learn more about 3D and VFX. It is such a huge field that being exclusively dedicated to Architecture Visualization felt very limiting.

After work, I would get home and spend hours studying particles, rigging, etc. For over a year, I was waking up an hour sooner to be able to dedicate some time to learning and practicing ZBrush, Human Anatomy.

At Arqui300, they made an effort to accommodate my interests and gave me as many opportunities as they could to put that extra knowledge into practice. They were also the ones who got me into teaching in the first place, something I became very passionate about and have been doing ever since one way or the other.

I have much to thank Arqui300.

Still, in 2011, I decided to go on my own to be more available for the type of projects I really wanted to be working on. Keep in mind that Portugal is a small country with not that many opportunities in VFX. The scene was dominated by a few main studios, and the connection with the outside world was not as fluent and accessible as it is today.

Still, I always managed to keep myself busy with my own projects, and through the publication of these, I never spent too much time without work. I can say that during my years as a freelancer, I've done everything you can think of in 3D at least once: from character design and animation to schoolbooks illustrations; from creating courses online to teaching on-site in universities; from assembling whole CG environments to doing camera tracking; from explosions to water simulations.

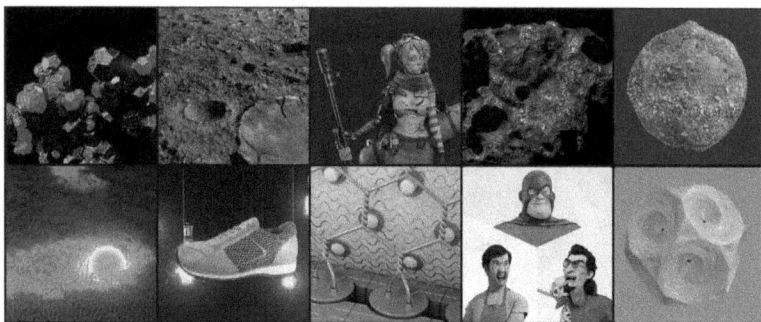

FIGURE 1.3   A sample of the different types of work I was doing.

I had the opportunity to work with many different clients and studios, so at a certain point I was very well established as someone who people would recommend for a broad range of tasks in the world of Computer Graphics. Still during those years, I had barely any experience working for film or tv productions.

In August 2019, I got my first real gig as a contracted freelancer for a VFX studio in Stuttgart, Germany, called Mackevision, working on a few productions that I knew me and millions of other people would be watching on TV.

My name was suggested by someone I had worked with in Portugal a few years back, on a freelance job for a studio in Lisbon. I later came to realize that this is actually the preferred way for a studio to hire someone new.

I spent that month in Stuttgart in the role of a Generalist, finding my way through the studio's pipeline and doing a bit of everything, from FX to shading, lighting, and rendering. I loved it more than I expected, which was surprising for me.

At the time of saying goodbye, they hinted at the possibility of having me come back again, and I was naturally very happy about that, not only because it meant I could revisit this world again but also because it meant I had done a good job.

They reached out to me a month later to know if I was interested in relocating to Stuttgart, Germany, under a no-term contract. After discussing it with my girlfriend, I said yes and started later that year on December 1, 2019.

A lot happened after that, including the death of my father, COVID, my return to Lisbon, and the birth of my son Cosmo.

Throughout that time, I kept working with Mackevision and climbed my way to the role of CG Supervisor starting with season 2 of Barbarians, a German production for Netflix, and season 2 of Foundation for Apple +.

I keep learning a lot about the role which comes with a lot of challenges and responsibilities but thanks to the amazing people I get to work with, it never stops being fun and exciting.

FIGURE 1.4   Real Playing Game—the Portuguese sci fi feature film production I worked on.

I also continue to do some freelance non-VFX work, I continue to teach, and the opportunity came up to write a book. I felt this could be an amazing way for me to share the knowledge and the insights I have acquired through my experience in this industry, to help guide others trying to figure out what they want to do.

FIGURE 1.5   Poster of the Watchmen series for HBO.

FIGURE 1.6 Mosaic of titles I've worked on at Mackevision.

FIGURE 1.7 Poster of Little Fan with all distinctions.

WHAT IS THIS BOOK ALL ABOUT

The goal of this book is to shed some light on the different roles and positions that make up the VFX industry at the scale of a VFX studio. Explaining what the responsibilities, common tasks, and skills required for each position are.

This alone is already of great value but I believe the biggest value of this book will be the sharing of stories of real people working in different positions of the industry with completely different paths and destinations. Getting access to their journey and their thoughts on their own journey should hopefully provide some support and encouragement to those considering starting from absolutely any point, to reach absolutely any target. As much as it may seem like a distant dream, reading about my story and the stories of these amazing people should demonstrate that whatever you're going for, it is within reach as long as you reach out for it.

Understanding the VFX Studio Ecosystem

2

The world of visual effects (VFX) is a complex ecosystem made up of various departments, teams, and roles that come together to create stunning visual content for films, television, and other media. For anyone aspiring to thrive in the VFX industry, it's very beneficial to have a clear understanding of how a VFX studio operates, the key departments involved, the hierarchy of positions, and the evolving landscape of VFX careers. This section will explore these areas in detail, helping you gain insights into the structure and dynamics of a VFX studio.

THE STRUCTURE OF A VFX STUDIO

A VFX studio is akin to a well-oiled machine, with numerous moving parts working in unison to bring visual effects to life. The size and structure of the studio can vary greatly depending on its scale, the projects it handles, and the clients it serves. At the highest level, VFX studios can range from small boutique shops specializing in niche services to global powerhouses that take on blockbuster movies and television shows.

A. **Types of VFX Studios:**
- **Boutique Studios**: These are smaller studios that typically focus on specific aspects of VFX such as modeling, compositing, or animation. Boutique studios are often sought after for their specialized expertise.
- **Full-Service Studios**: These studios offer end-to-end VFX solutions, from pre-production to post-production. They handle a wide range of tasks and are equipped to manage large-scale projects.

DOI: 10.1201/9781003494485-2

FIGURE 2.1   Closeup of a Pseudo Fractal structure—personal project.

FIGURE 2.2   Mosaic of main titles by ILM.

Here are five of the biggest VFX (Visual Effects) studios globally, along with their locations and estimated number of employees:

- **Industrial Light & Magic (ILM)**
  - **Location**: Headquarters in San Francisco, California, USA, with additional studios in Vancouver, London, Singapore, and Sydney.
  - **Estimated number of employees**: ~2,500+
  - **Notes**: Founded by George Lucas in 1975, ILM is a pioneer in the visual effects industry.
- **Weta Digital (now Wētā FX)**
  - **Location**: Wellington, New Zealand, with offices in Los Angeles and Vancouver.
  - **Estimated number of employees**: ~1,800+

- **Notes**: Renowned for work on films like *The Lord of the Rings* trilogy, *Avatar*, and more.
- **Framestore**
  - **Location**: Headquarters in London, UK, with additional studios in New York, Los Angeles, Montreal, and Mumbai.
  - **Estimated number of employees**: ~2,000+
  - **Notes**: Known for its work on movies like *Gravity*, *Guardians of the Galaxy*, and *Paddington*.
- **MPC (Moving Picture Company)**
  - **Location**: Headquarters in London, UK, with offices in Los Angeles, Bangalore, Montreal, Paris, and Adelaide.
  - **Estimated number of employees**: ~3,000+
  - **Notes**: Worked on films like *The Lion King* (2019), *The Jungle Book*, and *1917*.
- **DNEG (formerly Double Negative)**
  - **Location**: Headquarters in London, UK, with offices in Mumbai, Los Angeles, Vancouver, Montreal, and Chennai.

FIGURE 2.3   Mosaic of main titles by Weta FX (or Wētā FX).

FIGURE 2.4   Mosaic of main titles by Framestore.

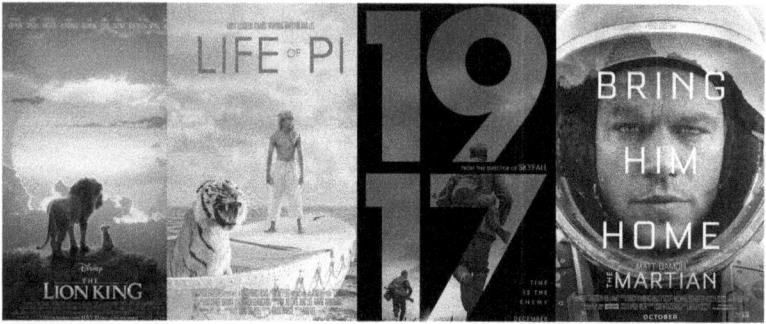

FIGURE 2.5   Mosaic of main titles by MPC.

FIGURE 2.6   Mosaic of main titles by DNEG.

- **Estimated number of employees**: ~7,000+
- **Notes**: DNEG has worked on films like *Inception, Interstellar,* and *Tenet.*

The studio I've been working on, Mackevision, has kept its original status as a boutique studio, offering very high-quality work and a wide range of services but keeping the structure small. For comparison, small means less than 100 people on staff, plus up to 30 freelancers during peak activity.

B. **Departments in a VFX Studio**: Each VFX studio is divided into departments responsible for different aspects of the VFX process. The typical departments include:
   - **Modeling**: This department creates the 3D models used in the production. Artists here are responsible for building the geometry/surfaces of characters, vehicles, props, and environments.

- **Texturing and Surfacing**: Once a model is created, the texturing department creates and/or applies textures and materials to those models to give them their final look, making them look realistic or stylized, depending on the project.
- **Lighting**: Lighting artists, in most cases, simulate real-world lighting to enhance the mood and depth of scenes, ensuring the final visuals appear natural and immersive. In some more creative productions, the realism is not as relevant, and the lighting artist ends up more in the role of a painter that works with light.
- **FX Simulation**: From explosions to water simulations, the FX team creates complex visual simulations that add realism to scenes. Again, depending on the production, the FX required may not have a real reference to adhere to and have to be imagined from scratch.
- **Rigging**: Responsible for creating the internal skeletons, or rigs, that allow 3D models—whether characters, creatures, or mechanical objects—to move in a realistic or nonrealistic and controlled manner.
- **Animation**: Character and object movement is brought to life by animators who apply principles of motion, emotion, and storytelling.
- **Compositing**: This department combines the visual elements into a cohesive scene, ensuring all the different parts blend seamlessly. This often includes combining real-life footage with multiple CG elements rendered in lighting.

KEY DEPARTMENTS AND THEIR ROLES

While each department has its specialized role, collaboration is key in VFX production. A comprehensive understanding of how these departments interact and depend on one another will help you navigate your career within the ecosystem. Here's a breakdown of the main roles within each department:

A. **Modeling Department**: Modelers are tasked with creating digital assets, working closely with concept artists and art directors to ensure that their creations align with the project's visual style.

B. **Texturing and Surfacing**: Artists here are responsible for giving models their surface appearance, working with lighting and rendering teams to ensure consistency across scenes.

C. **Rigging Department**: These are usually made up of technical artists that work in collaboration with both the modelers and the animators to design and implement joint systems, control points, and deformers that animators use to manipulate a model's movements, such as bending, stretching, or facial expressions. The rigging process ensures that models move naturally, allowing them to interact with their environment or perform specific actions in a believable way, essential for creating lifelike animations.

D. **Animation Department**: Animators breathe life into characters, creatures, and objects, focusing on movement and expression. They collaborate with riggers who create the skeletons or controls that animators use in production.

E. **FX Simulation**: FX artists work closely with the animation and compositing departments to create realistic effects, such as fire, water, smoke, and destruction; and also, nonrealistic effects such as the ones you often see in fantasy or sci fi themed productions

F. **Compositing Department**: Compositors are the final gatekeepers of the visual elements. They integrate all layers of the production, ensuring that the final images are cohesive and polished.

G. **Pipeline and Technical Roles**: To ensure smooth workflow between departments, technical artists and pipeline developers play a critical role. They create the tools and processes that allow teams to work efficiently and handle large data sets.

I. **Production**: The production team in a VFX studio is responsible for overseeing and managing the entire visual effects pipeline, ensuring that projects are completed on time, within budget, and to the desired quality standards. They coordinate communication between artists, supervisors, and clients, tracking progress, setting deadlines, and resolving any logistical or technical issues that arise. The production team also allocates resources, schedules tasks, and ensures that each department has what it needs to meet its goals. By maintaining a smooth workflow and addressing challenges promptly, they ensure that the VFX project runs efficiently from conception to final delivery.

THE HIERARCHY OF VFX POSITIONS

The VFX industry operates on a clear hierarchy, with various levels of responsibility and expertise. Understanding this hierarchy is essential for career progression.

A. **Junior Roles**:
  • **Junior Artist**: Fresh graduates or newcomers to the industry typically start in junior roles. These positions are designed

for learning and growing within the studio, often focusing on smaller tasks or assisting senior team members.

B. **Mid-Level Positions:**
- **Artist**: After gaining experience, junior artists progress to more independent roles, where they handle more complex tasks and larger portions of a project.
- **Lead Artist**: Lead artists oversee the work of other team members, ensuring consistency in style and quality. They are also responsible for troubleshooting and making creative decisions.

C. **Senior Roles:**
- **Senior Artist**: Senior artists have significant experience and are responsible for leading entire sections of a project. They often serve as mentors to junior team members.
- **Supervisors**: Department supervisors manage teams of artists and are responsible for ensuring that the work is on track, both creatively and technically. Supervisors must balance leadership, communication, and problem-solving skills.

D. **Executive Roles:**
- **VFX Supervisor**: VFX Supervisors have a comprehensive understanding of the entire pipeline. They oversee the entire visual effects process and work closely with directors, producers, and clients to ensure that the creative vision is realized.
- **VFX Producer**: Producers manage budgets, schedules, and client expectations. They ensure that the project stays on time and within financial constraints.

THE EVOLVING LANDSCAPE OF VFX CAREERS

The VFX industry is in constant flux, driven by advances in technology, changing production techniques, and the increasing demand for high-quality visual content. Here's how the landscape is evolving:

A. **Technological Advancements**:
- **AI and Machine Learning**: Artificial intelligence is transforming the way VFX artists work, from automating mundane tasks to creating more realistic simulations.
- **Virtual Production**: The rise of virtual production, using real-time rendering engines and LED walls, is changing how VFX is integrated into live-action filming, speeding up the production process and opening new career avenues.

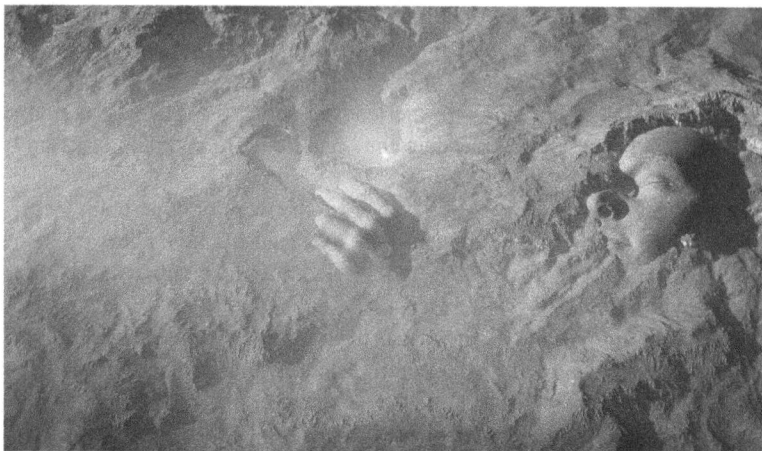

FIGURE 2.7   Alien Landscape—Frame capture of an animation I did while exploring UE.

- **Cloud Computing**: Cloud-based workflows are becoming more common, allowing studios to scale their operations and collaborate with talent globally.
- B. **The Rise of Streaming Services**: With the explosion of content on platforms like Netflix, Disney+, and Amazon Prime, there is an increasing demand for VFX-heavy series and films, resulting in more job opportunities and growth within the industry.
- C. **Globalization of VFX Work**: VFX production has become more global, with studios outsourcing work to different countries, creating a more distributed and flexible workforce.
- D. **Shifting Roles and Hybrid Artists**: Artists who possess a blend of creative and technical skills are becoming increasingly valuable. As the lines blur between different disciplines, studios are looking for hybrid artists who can wear multiple hats, adapting to various roles as needed.

This section sets the stage for a deeper dive into specific career paths and roles in the VFX industry, providing a solid foundation for understanding how VFX studios operate and what it takes to navigate a successful career in this exciting field.

The Journey to Becoming a CG Artist

3

FIGURE 3.1 Alien Landscape—Frame capture of an animation I did while exploring UE.

Becoming a Computer Graphics (CG) artist is a path that requires dedication, creativity, and continuous learning. Whether your goal is to work in films, games, or other digital media, the journey to becoming a successful CG artist is a blend of mastering technical skills while being creative plus developing a strong visual culture and understanding the industry. This section will guide you through the steps to start and grow your career, from acquiring the necessary skills to navigating early job roles in the VFX world.

DOI: 10.1201/9781003494485-3

BUILDING A FOUNDATION: EDUCATION AND SKILLS

The journey begins with education, but the routes to success as a CG artist are varied. Some professionals come from formal educational backgrounds, while others are self-taught. Regardless of your path, mastering the fundamentals is essential.

Do not underestimate the importance of a good foundation when learning something new. These may often seem too basic to be worth your time, and you may be tempted to skip them, but without those basic pieces, you'll always struggle more down the road because you'll have gaps in your foundations.

The area of CG, and especially applied in the VFX and Games industries, is broad enough to take advantage of whatever background you might have. I can say this from my own experience, my degree in Biology has provided me a basic understanding of scientific concepts that I didn't value at the time but have given me an advantage in understanding how ecosystems work and evolve and how I can recreate them with my own simplified algorithms to generate and manage large landscape environments or small particle systems.

My 3 years studying Architecture provided me with an understanding of geometry, volumes, visual harmony, the importance of light … all valuable knowledge when creating and lighting new worlds.

FIGURE 3.2   Frame capture from an animation I did as a personal project while exploring Houdini.

My interest in photography has also been invaluable in helping me understand how cameras work: Depth of Field, Motion Blur, Exposure, Refraction, …, all concepts a light and rendering artist uses or considers on a daily basis. So, whatever your background is, whatever experience you have acquired until the moment you decide you want to get into VFX, even if it seems a completely different direction then that you were going, you'll probably be able to make use of it at some point in your career in VFX.

Here are some of the more common paths.

A. **Formal Education:**
   • **Art and Design Schools**: Many aspiring CG artists start by attending art or design schools that offer specialized courses in animation, 3D modeling, and visual effects. These institutions provide a structured learning environment, access to industry-standard software, and opportunities for networking.
   • **Film and Game Design Programs**: Universities and colleges often have dedicated programs in film, game design, or digital media, providing a broader understanding of storytelling and production alongside CG skills.

B. **Self-Learning:**
   • **Online Courses and Tutorials**: Platforms like CGMA, FXPHD, Rebelway, Gnomon, Udemy, and YouTube offer a wealth of resources for learning CG techniques at your own pace. Many industry professionals have found success through self-taught methods, focusing on specialized areas such as character animation or environment design.
   • **Personal Projects**: One of the best ways to learn is by doing. Personal projects allow you to apply what you've learned, experiment with new techniques, and push your creative boundaries. These can be done alone but can be a much bigger learning experience if you find others on the same journey to collaborate with. This will not only allow you to develop your technical skills but also your soft skills which are essential when working in a studio environment, be it remotely or in situ. Plus, if you're dividing the load you can go for more ambitious projects.

C. **Essential Skills for a CG Artist:**
   • **Artistic Foundation**: A strong understanding of traditional art skills—such as composition, color theory, for some positions, also anatomy—will serve as a base for your digital work.
   • **Technical Proficiency**: CG artists must become proficient in industry-standard software like Houdini, Maya, Blender, Unreal

Engine, ZBrush, Nuke…this list can get quite long, especially considering how much there is to learn to master only one of these.

- **Problem-Solving**: The ability to creatively solve technical challenges is crucial in CG production, as each project will present unique problems to tackle.
- **Soft Skills**: This is a big one and not to be underestimated. Soft skills are crucial in a VFX studio environment because the work is highly collaborative, involving coordination between different departments, artists, and clients. Effective communication ensures that feedback is understood and implemented correctly, while teamwork fosters a supportive atmosphere where ideas can be shared, and challenges can be resolved together. Being receptive to feedback, maintaining a positive attitude, and managing stress contribute to a productive and creative work environment. Studios will usually prefer a less skilled artist in exchange for someone with the right attitude. Skills can be developed and acquired whereas character and professionalism will be harder if not impossible to teach.

THE ROLE OF A CG ARTIST

A CG artist's work varies depending on the project and the department they belong to. In some cases, you may be creating 3D models of characters or objects. In others, you may be designing lighting setups or creating complex visual effects.

You must have a clear understanding of the production pipeline and how your role interacts with other departments like animation, compositing, and lighting.

A. **Specializations:**
- **Modeling**: Creating 3D models that can be textured, rigged, and animated.
- **Texturing and Shading**: Applying textures to models to give them the desired look, whether it's photorealistic or stylized.
- **Lighting and Rendering**: Setting up lighting that enhances the mood of the scene and rendering the final image or sequence.
- **Animation**: Bringing characters and objects to life through movement, expressions, and dynamics.
- **FX**: Simulating elements like water, fire, smoke, and destruction to create realistic effects in the scene.

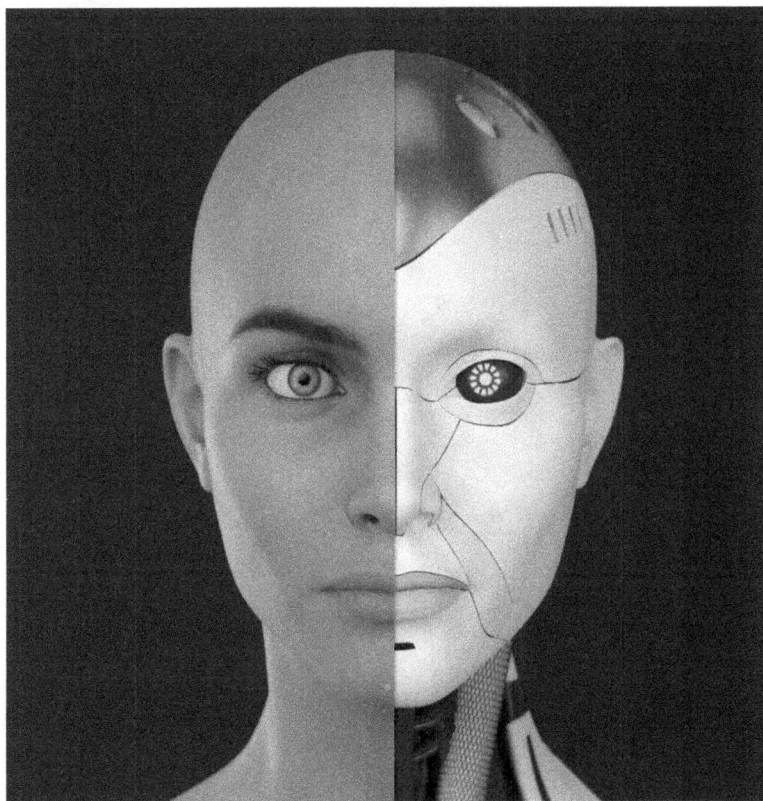

FIGURE 3.3 A cyborg character I had to create for a corporate presentation many years ago.

B. **Collaboration in a Studio Environment:**
- As a CG artist, you'll often work in teams, collaborating closely with other artists, supervisors, and departments. Strong communication skills and the ability to work well with others are essential to ensure that the final product meets the creative vision of the project.

DEVELOPING YOUR CG SKILLS

Becoming proficient as a CG artist is an ongoing process that doesn't stop after your initial education. The industry is always evolving, and staying on top of the latest tools and techniques is crucial for long-term success.

FIGURE 3.4 A character concept I created back in 2015.

A. **Mastering the Software:**
  - **3D Modeling Software**: 3D Studio Max, Maya, Blender, and ZBrush are the most common tools for 3D artists focused on modeling/sculpting. Understanding the nuances of these software packages, as well as keeping up with new features and updates, is important.
  - **Texturing Tools**: For artists working on texturing and/or shading, the main tools will be: Substance Painter from Adobe, or Mari from the Foundry. The Substance Suite started off as a great option for Game Development but has been progressively making its way into VFX with an ever-increasing capability to manage big assets with multiple high-resolution textures (UDIMs) per channel. Though Mari still remains the only viable option for the really high-end gigantic assets, since it can manage insane amounts of geo and textures very effectively.

- **Animation Tools**: If you plan to work as an animator, learning Maya, the industry-standard animation tool is essential. Houdini is becoming more and more attractive for the rigging and animation departments of VFX studios. With the latest release (Houdini 20.5) the concept of procedural rigging is becoming more accessible and offering highly complex and interesting animation options along with it. Anyone with an eye on **the** future and/or the cutting-edge animation systems available should invest more on the SideFX software.
- **FX Tools**: Houdini FX is by far the leader in this field. Without any need or dependency of third-party plugins, the default installation brings you all the tools you need to simulate realistic water, fire, destruction...at any scale. It also allows you to do particle simulations as complex as you can get them, along with a very robust and flexible crowd system.
- **Lighting and Rendering Tools**: Here you'll have a few different options, most of which are compatible with all main DCC (Digital Content Creation) tools. The main render engines currently in use for high-end VFX are RenderMan, Vray, Arnold, Karma, and Redshift. Karma is the newest of them all and is the new native render engine in Houdini since the 19.0 release. It's been evolving pretty well and its adoption growing, especially with the release of a full-featured XPU mode (meaning it can render with both GPU and CPU consistently). Redshift is mostly GPU focused, which comes with amazing speeds but also some limitations in terms of how much it can handle and also the quality of the final result when things get a bit more complex especially when including volumes. The three big ones—Renderman, Arnold, and Vray—will be a tradeoff between speed, ease of use, price, and subjective preference.
- **Production Tools**: There are two main players in this area: ShotGrid (formerly Shotgun) and FTrack. Plus, a third contender, which is NIM. ShotGrid (formerly Shotgun Software) is a widely used production management and collaboration tool specifically designed for VFX, animation, and game development. It provides robust tools for tracking tasks, managing assets, and overseeing the entire production pipeline, from pre-production to final delivery. FTrack is a cloud-based project management tool designed for the VFX, animation, and creative industries. It allows teams to track tasks, manage assets, review content, and collaborate efficiently. FTrack offers strong integration with major 3D and VFX software and is widely used for both small and large-scale productions. NIM is a production management

tool tailored for VFX, animation, and post-production work-flows. It offers features for tracking tasks, budgeting, client management, and asset management. NIM's focus is on providing a holistic solution that integrates both creative project tracking and business operations like finance and client relations. Anyone interested in production will greatly benefit from learning any of these options.

B. **Continuous Learning:**

This can be both seen as a curse and a blessing but there really is no way around it. On such a technological field the developments in hardware, software, and techniques happens at a very high pace. To be on the front, you really need to dedicate some time to keep yourself familiar with the latest trends and decide where to invest additional time to advance your career.

- **Workshops and Masterclasses**: There are always opportunities to sharpen your skills. Attending workshops, both online and in person, can give you direct access to industry experts and hands-on learning experiences.
- **Experimenting with New Techniques**: Every project offers an opportunity to try something new. Don't be afraid to experiment with techniques that challenge you or push your boundaries as an artist.

C. **Building Good Habits:**

- **Attention to Detail**: The best CG artists have an eye for detail, constantly refining their work until it matches the desired quality.
- **Iteration and Feedback**: Iterating on your work based on feedback is part of the CG process. Learning to accept and implement feedback from supervisors or clients is essential to growth.
- **Perfect is the Enemy of Good:** Striving for perfection can prevent progress or the completion of tasks, as perfectionists may spend excessive time and effort trying to make something flawless rather than accepting that "good enough" can often lead to success.

CREATING AN IMPRESSIVE REEL

In the VFX industry, the term portfolio is often replaced by either reel, demoreel, or showreel. The terms **demoreel** and **showreel** are often used interchangeably, but there can be subtle differences depending on context:

A. **Demoreel**: Typically refers to a compilation of work focused on demonstrating technical skills, especially in fields like VFX, animation, and 3D modeling. A demoreel is often used to showcase specific abilities in a particular software, pipeline, or technical role, such as rigging, compositing, or animation. It's more focused on presenting the candidate's craftsmanship and problem-solving abilities in their specialized area. Demoreels are usually the entry card for people seeking they're first opportunity in VFX.

B. **Showreel**: This term is more often used in the broader entertainment industry, including film, TV, acting, or directing. In VFX, it will usually be the same as a demoreel with the difference that the selected works come from real productions and not just demo projects. Showreels will usually be the presentation element for artists with already a few years of experience in the VFX industry. On showreels, it is essential that the artist specifies what their contribution was on each shot or asset. It is not uncommon to see showreels that are just a compilation of impressive VFX shots from different blockbusters, with no additional information. These are completely disregarded by studios, since they are left to guess what the artist's contribution was.

Your reel is your calling card in the VFX industry. It's what hiring managers and clients use to evaluate your skills, creativity, and versatility as an artist. A well-curated reel can make all the difference in landing your first job or advancing your career. Keep it concise, under two minutes, and ensure that it only contains your best work.

A. **Tailoring Your Reel to Your Career Path**:
- If you're aiming to become a modeler, focus your reel on showing a range of high-quality 3D models, emphasizing different styles and complexity. For animators, showcasing your understanding of movement, weight, and emotion is key.
- Ensure that your portfolio aligns with the kind of work you want to do. If your goal is to work in feature films, your portfolio should highlight your abilities in high-quality, polished work.

B. **What to Include:**
- **Diverse Work**: Showcasing a variety of skills is important. Include both technical and artistic projects to highlight your versatility.
- **Breakdowns**: Include breakdowns of how you approached certain tasks, showing your problem-solving process and technical expertise.

- **Personal Projects**: These can highlight your creative drive and passion, as well as your ability to manage a project from start to finish.

C. **Online Presence:**
  - Having an online portfolio or website where potential employers can easily view your work is crucial. Platforms like ArtStation, Behance, and Vimeo can help you showcase your portfolio to a wider audience.

NAVIGATING INTERNSHIPS AND JUNIOR CG ROLES

Breaking into the industry often starts with internships or junior roles. These opportunities allow you to gain real-world experience, develop industry contacts, and learn the intricacies of working in a studio environment.

A. **Finding Internships**:
  - **Industry Connections**: Networking is key to finding internships. Attend industry events, join online communities, and reach out to professionals for advice or potential opportunities. This is one of the main advantages of following a school

FIGURE 3.5   Frame capture from a personal project animation.

learning path, since you get to connect with and gain direct access to VFX professionals that can help you to get your first opportunity. Some schools actually use this as a marketing tool by offering career guidance and internships at studios with which the school has established connections and protocols.

- **Applying for Internships**: When applying, tailor your resume and reel to the studio's needs. Highlight relevant skills and show that you're eager to learn.

B. **Maximizing Your Internship Experience:**

- **Being Proactive**: Internships are as much about learning as they are about contributing. Take the initiative to ask questions, seek feedback, and offer help where needed. This shows your commitment and can lead to more significant responsibilities.

- **Learning the Studio Pipeline**: Every studio has a unique pipeline, and learning how things work at each stage of production will give you an edge in future roles. It may seem something you won't need except if you actually end up working at that studio, but all studios have the same essential needs in terms of pipeline. Even if the interfaces and processes are a bit different you will still have to know how to do the same basic pipeline tasks anywhere you go. Another reason for making an effort to learn the pipeline is that it may allow for you to become more relevant at another studio where you might be able to make suggestions of how to improve the pipeline.

C. **Moving from Junior Roles to Mid-Level:**

- Once you've gained some experience as an intern or junior artist, you can begin to take on more complex tasks. Continue building your skills, refining your reel, and seeking mentorship from senior artists or supervisors.

- Pay attention to the areas of the production process that interest you most. Specializing in a particular role can help you move up the ranks more quickly, whether that's becoming a lighting artist, FX artist, or modeler.

The Jobs

4

The VFX industry offers a variety of specialized roles, each contributing a unique skill set to the production pipeline. Understanding the different jobs available is essential for anyone looking to enter the field or specialize in a specific area. This section breaks down the most common roles within VFX, providing an overview of what each position entails, the skills required, and how to excel in these roles.

MODELER

The journey of creating a 3D asset begins with the modeler and the same can be said about the journey of many VFX careers since this is usually where you start when learning a 3D software. As a modeler, your job is to take a concept or design and bring it into the three-dimensional space. Whether it's a character, an environment, or an object/prop, modelers are responsible for building the surface and volume that will give shape to these elements.

There are different modeling techniques:

- **Classic Poly Modeling**—the modeler creates and manipulates points, edges, and polygons to build the model. Because this type of modeling is the oldest of all the types presented here, it's not surprising that the list of most commonly used software shows some of the oldest DCCs still around: 3Ds Max is usually preferred to Maya; Blender is a really good option; while ZBrush and Houdini also offer evolving tools and interfaces for traditional poly modeling.
- **Sculpting**—the modeler works with virtual clay like materials and tools, recreating the traditional sculpting techniques but taking it to a whole new level that only the virtual world makes possible. Because the modeler doesn't really need to pay much attention to the point

DOI: 10.1201/9781003494485-4

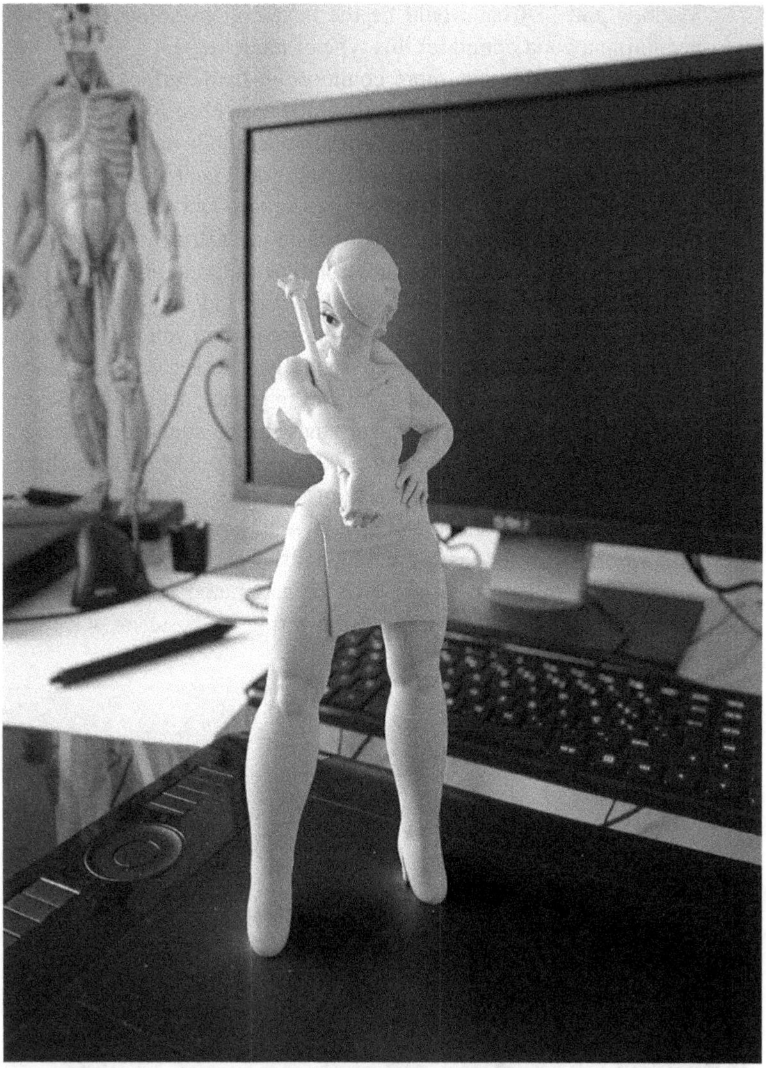

FIGURE 4.1 Personal project as a modeling/sculpting exercise with integration on my desk.

count or total polygons, this often requires some optimization in the final stage when the model is approved. Whether to make it deform correctly, for instance, sculpting a character to be animated, or to just reduce the total number of polys to reduce the resources it will require for rendering. Sculpting is strongly dominated by ZBrush.

Mudbox and 3DCoat would be the next options. Blender is also becoming a good option for this type of modeling.

- **Boolean Modeling**—is more common on hard surface elements. You can create extremely complex shapes with a lot of intricate detail by combining different shapes in operations of addition, subtraction, intersection, ... The resulting model isn't as high density as the raw output from a sculpting approach but the topology is often messy and also requires some clean up. ZBrush, Blender, and Houdini provide great options for this type of modeling.
- **Procedural Modeling**—this is a very vast field with infinite possibilities. This approach is more often used when you need a lot of variations of the same object. Essentially, you set up a sequence of rules and operations that result in an object, let's say a chair. Then you expose a few parameters that can be adjusted to change the resulting object. In the chair example, it could be something like, allowing the person using the tool to control the number of legs, height of seat, shape and size of seat, height of the back, ... This would allow for easily creating a series of different chairs very quickly, and this process can even be automated by randomizing those parameters and saving out the result for posterior selection

FIGURE 4.2   One of my first 3D projects during my Architecture graduation.

of preferred versions. I gave the example of a chair, but this can be taken a lot further and both in the realm of hard surface modeling but also organic modeling. The typical software used here would be Houdini or Blender.

The selection of the approach will depend on the element being modeled and if it will be later deformed or if it's a static mesh.

The modelers vocabulary include points, vertices, edges, polygons, triangles, loops, booleans, topology, uvs, and a few other terms that pop up on a daily basis.

A. **Responsibilities:**
- Create 3D models based on concept art or references, ensuring that they meet the project's technical and artistic requirements.

FIGURE 4.3 Animal anatomy sculpting exercise.

- Collaborate with the texturing, rigging, and animation departments to ensure the models work properly throughout the pipeline.
- Make adjustments based on feedback from art directors, supervisors, or clients to refine the models for use in production.

FIGURE 4.4   Doctrisch—A character I developed as a personal project from concept to final 3D render.

B. **Skills Needed:**
   - **Technical Proficiency**: Mastery of 3D modeling software such as Maya, Blender, and ZBrush is essential.
   - **Understanding of Anatomy and Structure**: Particularly for character modeling, a solid understanding of anatomy, weight distribution, and muscle structure is vital.
   - **Attention to Detail**: You'll need a keen eye for detail to ensure that models are accurate and realistic or stylized as required.

C. **Career Growth:**
   - Junior modelers typically start with simple assets and gradually move on to more complex models as they gain experience.
   - Specializing in specific areas, like character modeling, vehicle modeling, or environment modeling, can lead to more advanced roles such as lead modeler or even modeling supervisor.

D. **Me as a Modeler**

   Like most people working in the 3D side of things, I started learning 3D by learning how to model. Since I started in the Architecture context, it's not surprising that my first models were converting 2D Autocad projects from my first year's Projects class into full 3D models in 3D Studio Max.

That might have been the start of it, but it certainly wasn't the end. I dedicated a lot of time to drawing and studying anatomy.

Many hours practicing Sculpting in ZBrush. I had a lot of fun and still earned a good amount of money as a 3D character developer.

FIGURE 4.5 Personal Project based on procedural modeling and shading complex rock structures.

Eventually transitioning to VFX and Houdini made my modeling skills to focus almost exclusively on procedural modeling.

To this day, even in the role of CG Supervisor I still take on some artist tasks where my procedural modeling skills are quite useful, especially on the creation and management of big assets or environments.

SURFACING ARTIST

Once the model is complete, the surfacing artist steps in to bring it to life through textures and materials. Surfacing artists, also known as texture artists or shading artists, are responsible for defining the visual details of the models, from skin textures to fabric, metal, and beyond.

The development of textures can also be done through many different ways. Here are some of the most common:

- **Vertex Painting**—It is a texturing technique that relies on applying color information to points, so it is very much dependent on the model's resolution and is more suitable for models coming from a sculpting approach. It is very fast and responsive, and it doesn't

FIGURE 4.6　Car rendering I did for a Vray demo course.

even require UVs, but it does require a lot of geometry to be able to paint smaller details. This information can then be converted/baked to a regular 2D texture. Most main DCCs will support this type of texturing but the main software used with this technique is ZBrush.

• **UV Projection Painting**—This approach makes use of the model's UVs to directly project the painting actions to 2D textures. You are able to get a lot of detail applied to even extremely low-resolution models. Though the painting gestures are very fluid and detailed, this does require an additional operation to take place which is the actual projection of the action in screen space to the actual UV space of the model. Depending on the resolution and UDIM count of the model, this operation can vary between being completely unnoticeable to taking a few seconds on more demanding models. The main players on this field are Substance Painter and for more high-end VFX productions, Mari. Houdini also started supporting this type of projection painting from its 20.5 release.

• **Procedural Texturing**—This approach makes use of some characteristics of the model's shape and geometry to generate automatic masks from its features which can then be combined with regular textures to create something that looks very realistic and tailor-made for the model. Some of the most common features used in this process are Ambient Occlusion, Curvature, Thickness, Surface Normals direction, and World Position. This approach can be combined with any of the previously mentioned and can be developed at geometry level and/or shader level which means it will also be dependent on the render engine being used. Both Substance Painter and Mari provide a lot of options for this. Also, any of the main render engines will also provide tools for this type of shading.

The Surfacing Artist's vocabulary includes UVs, UDIMs, color space, channels, PBR, dielectric, metallic, resolution, IOR, white balance, value, hue, saturation, gamma, and a few more.

A. **Responsibilities:**
   • Apply textures, colors, and materials to 3D models, ensuring that they look realistic or meet the artistic direction of the project.
   • Work closely with the lighting and rendering teams to ensure that the textures behave properly under different lighting conditions.
   • Use software like Substance Painter, Mari, and Photoshop to create high-quality texture maps.

B. **Skills Needed:**
- **Texturing and Shading**: A strong grasp of different texturing techniques.
- **Artistic Eye**: An understanding of color theory, material properties, and surface detail is essential for creating believable and visually appealing textures.
- **Technical Knowledge**: Familiarity with UV mapping, procedural texturing techniques, and how shaders function within the rendering pipeline.

C. **Career Growth:**
- Surfacing artists can progress to senior positions, lead roles, or even specialize further in specific areas like photorealism or stylized textures. As with other roles, collaboration with other departments is key to long-term success.

D. **Me as a Surfacing Artist**

I believe most modelers will eventually delve into surfacing so they can better display their models. Even if a great model only needs good lighting to be properly displayed, in a lot of situations, the texturing and surfacing are essential to tell everything you need to know about the element being modeled. Be it a character, a vehicle, or a prop. Just imagine a character with a glass eye. If displayed solely in clay shade, you will never know that one of the character's eyes is actually made of glass.

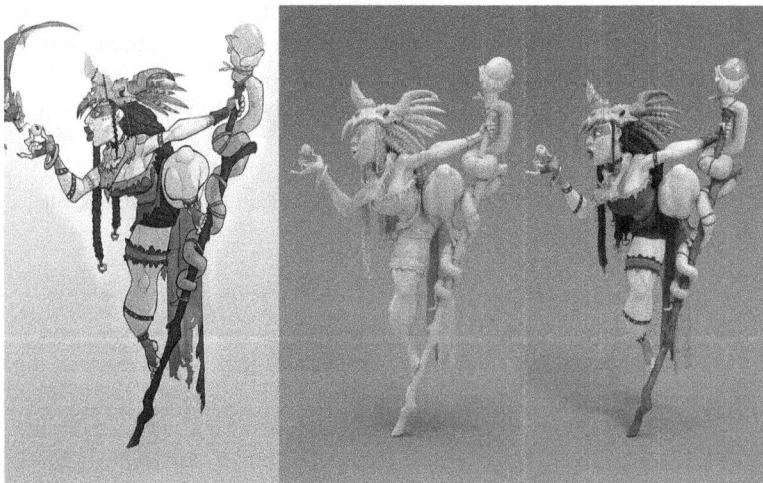

FIGURE 4.7   Witch—Personal work based on an amazing concept I found in a book.

My first texturing jobs were actually done in Photoshop for that first free-lance gig that changed my life. I was grabbing photos and unwrapping low poly models of entire streets in Macau, then stitching everything together purely in 2D inside Photoshop. This was, of course, long before Google Earth or Google Maps, probably even before Google itself.

When I started using Mudbox and ZBrush, I really enjoyed polypainting for creating my textures. But from early on I was rendering my works in 3D Studio Max with Vray and combining textures with procedural techniques to get more out of my texturing work.

I also used Mari for a while, mostly because it was the most advanced high-end texturing tool available, and I basically wanted to do it like the big boys and girls were doing it especially for painting realistic skin textures.

Then Substance Painter came out and started to go a bit beyond the game industry. When it was able to output 4k textures, it really became a real, more intuitive, and cheaper alternative to Mari.

The whole Substance ecosystem had a huge boom at some point, and you can see absolutely incredible examples of procedural texture generation taking Substance Designer to the limit.

And because I loved procedural even before I was aware of it, I also made some incursions in that field.

Nowadays working mostly as a CG Supervisor, I still take on some tasks from other roles among which will inevitably be some shading tasks. My approach tends to be as procedural as possible since it gives me a lot of flex-ibility. This will be particularly useful when you're starting, for instance, an

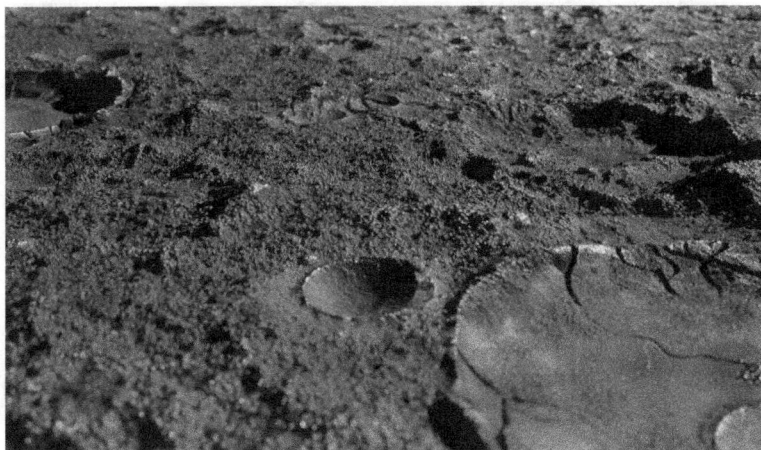

FIGURE 4.8   Asteroid Surface created procedurally with Substance Designer.

environment that no one has ever seen before like the landscape of an alien planet. The amount of iterations and changes that you'll go through on an asset like this requires speed and efficiency, if you were to be dependent on manual work to build something like this you would require a lot more work hours. Having procedural shaders is a way to make sure that even if the layout of the landscape changes, the shape of a mountain, the size of a ship, the shaders will automatically adapt and still look good.

LIGHTING AND RENDERING ARTIST

Lighting artists play a crucial role in setting the mood and atmosphere of a scene. They are responsible for ensuring that the lighting within a scene not only enhances the visual appeal but also meets the narrative needs of the project.

Each render engine will come with a set of capabilities and limitations, so besides having to master the lighting and rendering options provided by the render engine, a lighting and rendering artist also needs to be able to optimize the different scenes and adapt to the hardware resources available. The most common constraints will be RAM and/or VRAM, number of render nodes, and, of course, time.

FIGURE 4.9 Frame capture from an animation I did while exploring UE.

Although we're constantly seeing improvements in the hardware and software used for creating VFX, the tendency is to also expect to be able to do more, better, and faster, so you're always going as close to the limit as possible.

A. **Responsibilities:**
   - Set up and adjust lighting to enhance the visual storytelling, mood, and tone of scenes in films, commercials, or games.
   - Collaborate compositing teams to ensure that they have everything they need to produce the final look of the shot.
   - Work with a variety of lighting and rendering tools within softwares like Maya and Houdini using render engines like Arnold, Karma, Vray, and Redshift to achieve the desired look.
   - Making sure that the scene actually renders at full resolution and final quality.

B. **Skills Needed:**
   - **Knowledge of Lighting Techniques**: Understanding how light behaves in real life and how to simulate these behaviors in 3D environments is essential. This includes knowledge of global illumination, reflections, shadows, and volumetric lighting.
   - **Artistic and Technical Balance**: Lighting artists must blend technical know-how with artistic sensibility, ensuring that scenes are both visually compelling and technically accurate.
   - **Collaboration**: Lighting is one of the final stages of the VFX pipeline, so you'll need to collaborate closely with other departments, especially surfacing and compositing, to ensure that the final output matches the artistic vision.

C. **Career Growth:**
   - Starting as a junior lighting artist, you'll move up by handling more complex scenes or whole sequences and learning how to troubleshoot technical issues. Senior lighting artists often take on more creative responsibilities and may progress to supervisory roles. It's one of the most common routes to get to CG Supervisor, where your work becomes a mix of executing, supervision, and production.

D. **Me as a Lighting and Rendering Artist**

My first real lighting and rendering jobs were done in the ArchViz context. When I started, I didn't have much knowledge on lighting principles. I analyzed high-quality archviz images and followed amazing artists, but it wasn't easy for me to figure out why a certain image looked so good and others, like my own, looked so bland. Looking at architecture, photography made it a bit easier and also having the chance to work alongside really talented people at my first job at Arqui300 made a big difference. Despite the obvious evolution, I never saw myself as a talented lighting artist, and there was so much more to explore in the CG universe that I just shifted my focus to other areas. With time I did get a lot better. As much as you might want to speed things up and put in as many hours as possible, the truth is that there is a point where time and experience become the essential ingredients to keep growing. Everyone will benefit from time and experience differently. Under the same starting point and conditions, some will take longer than others to reach a new level. Maybe natural aptitude or genetics play a role in this, but I believe the main differentiator will be the attitude and commitment. Someone who takes criticism well, who will put in the work to overcome a difficulty, who is receptive to feedback, who won't be afraid of asking questions, can go through a transformative process of growth and evolution especially in a studio environment. Hence, the value studios give to that component when considering hiring someone.

FIGURE 4.10   Personal work done as a VRay demo while teaching at a school in Lisbon.

I wasn't always like that. I've always seen myself as a committed, reliable, and professional artist but when I was younger I sometimes took feedback too personally and also had to grow as a person to become a better professional.

Lighting and rendering is a very common task for me nowadays. I still don't think I'm amazing at it, which becomes super clear when working alongside amazing lighting artists, but I do a decent job.

FX ARTIST

FX artists are the magicians behind the scenes, creating elements like fire, water, explosions, smoke, and other dynamic visual effects. This is one of the most technically demanding roles in VFX, requiring a blend of physics simulation and artistic creativity. The FX artists also need to be great problem solvers, since along with common tasks like explosions, there will be many situations where they are asked to create something that no one has ever seen before just based on a text description or a still image.

This space is currently dominated by Houdini from Side FX. The default installation of Houdini FX comes with some of the most advanced tools for creating natural and fantastic FX out of the box without the need for any additional Third-Party plugins, as it was so common a few years ago when these FX were still developed in Maya and 3D Studio Max.

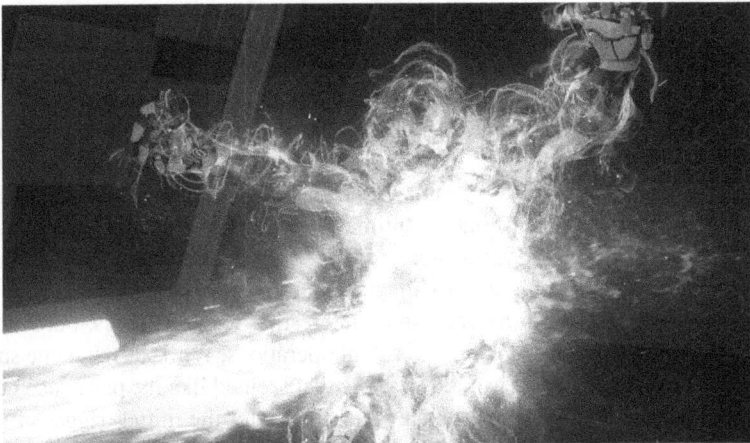

FIGURE 4.11 Frame capture of an animation I did to promote a course on CG Circuit.

A. **Responsibilities:**
- Simulate and create visual effects that enhance the story, using particle systems, dynamics, and fluid simulations to achieve realistic effects.
- Work closely with the compositing and lighting teams to integrate the effects seamlessly into the final shots.
- Use tools such as Houdini, RealFlow, and Maya to create complex simulations for smoke, fire, water, and destruction effects.

B. **Skills Needed:**
- **Technical Mastery**: FX artists need to have a strong understanding of physics, particle systems, and simulations. Familiarity with advanced tools and techniques, and with one or more programming languages, is critical for success in this role.
- **Creative Problem-Solving**: Creating effects that fit within the visual style of a project can be challenging. You'll need to find innovative solutions to technical challenges while maintaining the desired artistic direction.
- **Attention to Realism**: Whether the project demands realistic or stylized effects, FX artists need to be able to craft simulations that feel believable and cohesive within the scene.

C. **Career Growth:**
- FX artists often move into lead and supervision FX roles, where they manage teams and take on more complex shots. There are also opportunities to specialize further in specific effects, such as water or destruction simulations.

D. **Me as an FX Artist**

It didn't take me too long to become interested in FX. It started with Particle Flow in 3Ds Max, then After Burn from Sitni Sati, which worked with regular particles and sprites to create volume like effects for explosions and clouds. Later Sitni Sati released Fume FX which allowed for actual volume simulations inside 3D Studio Max to create more sophisticated explosions and fire simulations. This was my introduction to concepts like Volume Grids, advection, fields, etc., really cool stuff but quite time consuming and memory intensive.

Thinking Particles was a more advanced particles system from Cebas. This plugin was probably my first introduction to some procedural concepts. Particle Flow already introduced some interesting logic concepts, but it still followed a very unidirectional sequence of operations. While as the name suggests, Thinking Particles, worked in a way that seemed like the particles knew how to behave at any given moment. Meaning, after the initial trigger of the simulation everything was condition dependent and that required that the particles were more aware of what was happening around them. At the time, this was the preferred system for RBD simulations and fracturing.

Inevitably, after exploring earth, air, and fire, I started to get curious about water as well. The main fluid simulation tool at the time was Realflow. The interface alone screamed Advanced Level, with the dark viewport, blue particles, and wireframe geometry display. It was at this time that I started to first learn some Python. The default tools and solvers were great but if you knew how to code, you could really take your sims to the next level.

My FX journey would eventually lead me to Houdini. Around 2016 Houdini started to come up more and more in my feeds and on YouTube. I investigated a bit, and it seemed absolutely insane. A completely different way of working in 3D for someone used to 3D Studio Max. I still remembered how alien ZBrush felt in the beginning as well, until after a while everything just made a lot of sense. And I was just too infatuated with Houdini to be intimidated by a new way of doing things, especially considering the things I would be able to do. It was just too interesting and too much of a challenge for me to resist it. It requires a lot of determination. When you're already really good with a tool, the idea of going back to level 1 with a tool that will let you do the same things (and much more) is not easy. The temptation to just postpone the transition and go back to the tool where you'll be able to perform the same task 5 times faster is pretty big. Looking back now, I'm really glad; I decided to make that shift when I did. It allowed me to be better prepared for the future and brought me a lot of amazing opportunities like writing this book.

Only thinking about this now, as I write, I become aware of the crazy journey I've gone through to get to where I am today.

RIGGER

Riggers create the skeletal structures that animators use to move characters, creatures, and objects. Rigging is a highly technical role that combines knowledge of anatomy, mechanical design, and programming to ensure that models move fluidly and realistically.

A. **Responsibilities:**
- Build and implement rigs for characters, vehicles, or any other object that requires movement. This includes creating the underlying control systems that allow animators to manipulate the models.
- Work closely with animators to ensure that the rigs are functional and meet the creative requirements of the project.
- Solve technical issues related to deformation, movement, and rig performance within the animation pipeline.
- Solve technical issues related to the export of the animated assets so they can be easily imported by the Light and Render Department.

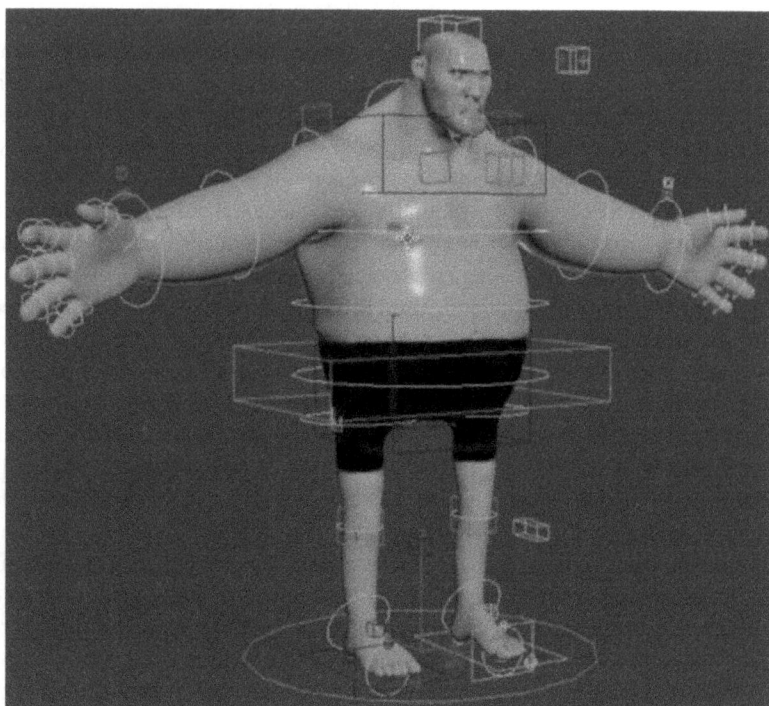

FIGURE 4.12   Rigged character using my own auto rig plugin. For a personal project that I never finished.

B. **Skills Needed:**
- **Understanding of Anatomy**: For character rigging, a deep understanding of anatomy and muscle movement is crucial to create realistic rigs that animate naturally.
- **Technical Knowledge**: Proficiency in rigging tools within Maya, Blender, or Houdini, as well as scripting languages like Python or MEL for automating repetitive tasks.
- **Problem-Solving**: Rigging often requires troubleshooting technical issues and developing custom tools to meet specific project needs.

C. **Career Growth:**
- Riggers can advance to senior or lead rigging positions and may also branch into technical direction or character technology roles, overseeing larger technical aspects of a production.

D. **Me as a Rigger**

As you're probably already guessing by now, I also went through a rigger phase. At the time, I was already at a pretty advanced level of 3D Studio Max and comfortable with MaxScript. I spent a few months working on developing an Auto Rig tool which I named Monkey Rig. Even though I got it into a pretty advanced stage I never officially released a version to the public.

I used it a few times on personal projects which was great for testing it in real production and making improvements to the tool but after a few interruptions (to attend to paying jobs jobs), it ended up staying in the drawer for too long and me moving on to other things.

Still, like with everything else I explored, I carried on a lot of concepts, knowledge, and experience that would help me later on my transition to Houdini and to becoming a true Generalist.

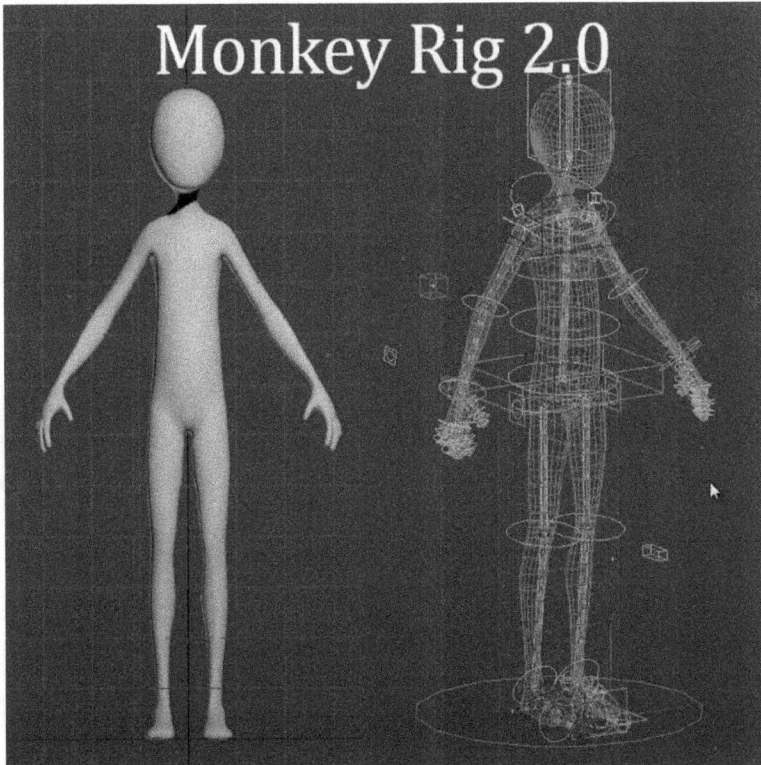

FIGURE 4.13   Promotional image for my 3Ds MAx auto rig tool called Monkey Rig.

ANIMATOR

Animators bring characters and objects to life, creating the motion and behavior that gives VFX and CG work its emotional depth. Whether it's animating creatures, vehicles, or facial expressions, animators are at the heart of storytelling in VFX.

A. **Responsibilities:**
   - Create animations for characters or objects that convey motion, emotion, and action in line with the project's requirements.
   - Work with riggers to ensure that the rigs allow for smooth and realistic movement, while also addressing technical issues that may arise during animation.
   - Collaborate with the directors and supervisors to match the style and pacing of the animation to the broader narrative.

B. **Skills Needed:**
   - **Understanding of Motion and Timing**: Knowledge of how things move in real life and applying that understanding to animated characters or objects.
   - **Creativity and Emotional Expression**: Whether it's subtle facial expressions or dynamic action sequences, animators need to inject emotion and creativity into their work to make it compelling.

FIGURE 4.14   Frame capture from an animation I did with a putterfish.

- **Software Proficiency**: Mastery of animation tools such as Maya is essential for success in this role. Houdini is making great strides to become a real alternative to Maya in this area as well.
C. **Career Growth:**
   - Animators often begin by working on simpler tasks and progress to more complex shots, eventually leading teams as senior animators or animation supervisors. Some animators also move into directing roles in animation or VFX.
D. **Me as an Animator**

I experimented with some animation tasks on my personal projects. Since most of those projects were a one-man show, I didn't really have much of a choice. After doing all the character development, including rigging, it's absolutely amazing when you get to the part of actually giving life to those characters through motion and emotion. But it was probably the area where I spent the least amount of time. Can't really say why but I guess I was always eager to finally light and render the work so I could show it to people.

COMPOSITOR

Compositors are responsible for bringing together all the different elements of a shot—whether it's live-action footage, CG models, or special effects—and making them look like one cohesive image. This is one of the final steps in the VFX process, requiring both artistic skill and technical know-how. Even today I'm often surprised with how much you can do in Compositing. It is an area where the integration of cutting-edge technology happens the fastest. Maybe because so much of the work is concentrated on a single software—Nuke. The second contender—DaVinci Resolve still does an amazing job to keep up and can even get ahead in some topics.

A. **Responsibilities:**
   - Combine CG elements, live-action footage, matte paintings, and other assets into final shots, ensuring that everything fits seamlessly.
   - Adjust lighting, color, and other visual elements to match the overall tone of the scene and maintain continuity.
   - Work closely with the FX, lighting, and rendering teams to make sure all elements come together in the final composition.

FIGURE 4.15   Another Vray demo project from my years as a teacher.

B. **Skills Needed:**
   - **Technical Knowledge**: Proficiency in software such as Nuke or DaVinci Resolve is essential, as is an understanding of color correction, rotoscoping, and green screen keying.
   - **Attention to Detail**: Compositors must ensure that all visual elements match perfectly, from lighting and shadows to perspective and scale.
   - **Artistic Sensibility**: Beyond the technical aspects, compositors need a strong artistic eye to ensure that the final image is visually compelling.

C. **Career Growth:**
   - Compositors can move into senior roles or lead positions, eventually becoming compositing supervisors. Some may also transition into VFX supervision, where they oversee the entire visual effects process.

D. **Me as a Compositor**

My Compositor formation started in After Effects which I believe will be the entry point for a lot of people. Especially if you're already familiar with Photoshop and working with static images. Also, because the cost is just a very small fraction and despite the limitations of a layer/track-based approach, it also has a lot of development put into it and a huge community. At the time, the Video Copilot was probably my main source of knowledge, and you can have lots of fun capturing your own footage and then applying those tutorials to it.

Eventually, I moved on to Fusion, again trying to follow the big players under the assumption that "if that's how they do it then it must really be the best way." For someone coming from After Effects, it takes a bit to get used to, but it really is the best way to do it. Not necessarily for very simple things but for more complex scenes it's undisputable. Then I tried Nuke which was a much easier adaptation after getting used to the node-based approach in Fusion. Just a matter of learning new names for the same tools.

I was applying all of this knowledge in my own projects. Not just the full cg ones but for a while I dedicated myself to integrating my 3D work in real life footage. My girlfriend had a nice DSLR with some good lenses, so I would go out, film, do a 360 multi stop capture of the location, then go home, stitch the HDRi together with PTGui, do the Camera tracking in Syntheyes, undistort the plate, render some FX and put it all together in Fusion or Nuke, plus some additional Color Grading and final look dev in After FX. Madness but really lots of fun.

I believe it is essential for a lighting and rendering artist to know how to do basic compositing. That's the only way to know what you need to render to get to the final image. Most people will assume we render everything together but that's very rarely the case. In most situations, it will provide a lot more control and flexibility if you render things in layer and combine everything in compositing. Having some basic compositing skills will give the lighting and rendering artist the chance to do some look dev in comp and apply the adjustments or style options back to the 3D before the next iteration. These look experiments are much faster to do in 2D than in 3D, so that is a big plus. Also, this knowledge will make the communication with the Compositing department a lot easier.

The Generalist

5

In the VFX industry, many artists choose to specialize in a single discipline, like modeling, animation, or lighting, while others opt for a broader skill set that spans multiple areas. These multi-talented professionals are known as generalists. A generalist possesses skills across various aspects of the VFX pipeline, allowing them to contribute flexibly within teams or handle diverse tasks independently. This section explores the role of the generalist, including the skills needed, the advantages and challenges of this career path, and how to succeed as an adaptable artist in the ever-evolving VFX landscape.

ARTIST UNIVERSALIS—DEFINING THE CG GENERALIST

Much like the concept of *uomo universalis* or Renaissance Man, the CG Generalist will be someone who believes in their limitless development capacity and is ready to assimilate all knowledge. Or they're just someone who can't make up their mind on what they want to do so they try everything.

In a world of specialists, the CG generalist stands out for their versatility. While they may not delve as deeply into specific techniques as a specialist, generalists bring a unique set of strengths to a project, offering flexibility and a holistic view of the entire production pipeline.

A. **What is a CG Generalist?**
- A CG generalist has proficiency across multiple areas in VFX, such as modeling, texturing, lighting, basic animation, and often also coding. They might not reach the depth of a specialist in any single area but are skilled enough to handle various tasks effectively.

 DOI: 10.1201/9781003494485-5

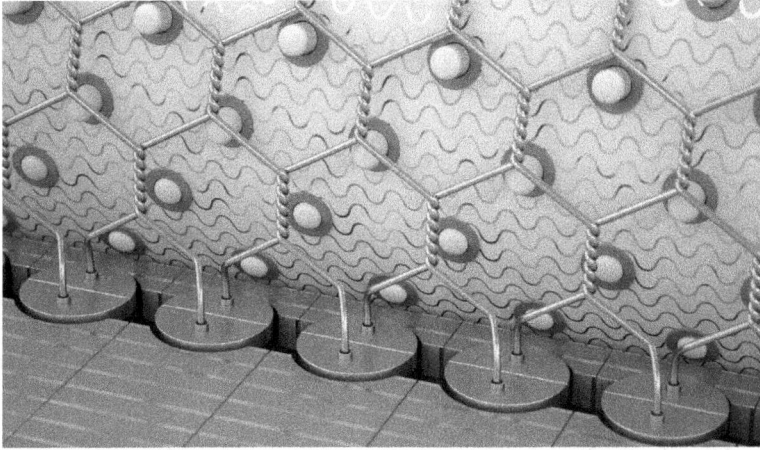

FIGURE 5.1 Frame capture from an animation I did based on a real fence-making machine. All done procedurally in Houdini.

- Generalists are often called upon in smaller studios where specialized roles may not exist. In larger studios, they may work in departments that require broader skill sets, such as previsualization, and scene assembly, or smaller VFX teams within a larger production.

B. **Roles and Responsibilities:**
- Generalists are often responsible for creating full assets or scenes, handling them from start to finish. This includes modeling, texturing, shading, lighting, and rendering.
- They may also be involved in troubleshooting and assisting specialized teams when projects require additional support across multiple disciplines.

C. **Key Characteristics of a Successful Generalist**:
- **Adaptability**: The ability to switch between tasks and skills as needed.
- **Holistic Understanding**: A well-rounded view of the VFX pipeline, allowing them to foresee how their work will impact other departments.
- **Problem-Solving**: Generalists often tackle a range of tasks, requiring a knack for quickly finding solutions to diverse technical and artistic challenges.
- **Good Communication**: Because of their broad knowledge across multiple disciplines, they are often assigned a flexible role that requires communication between multiple departments.

LEARNING EVERYTHING

Becoming a successful generalist involves developing a broad skill set, which requires dedication, time, and effective learning strategies. I would emphasize the time component. It's not enough to go through all the content and understand it, you will need to put it to practice several hours a day for a good number of consecutive days in order to become proficient in any given topic. To become a Generalist, you'll have to do this through multiple topics. And as you build up your skill set, you'll have to dedicate time to learning the new skills and also to maintaining the skills you already have. Generalists must continually refine their knowledge across multiple disciplines, making their education a unique and ongoing journey.

Most Generalists will probably say they didn't really have a plan to become a Generalist, it just happens naturally for people with a certain profile.

In my case, from what I consider today to be the minimum level a professional should have to be a Generalist, I would say it took me 8 years, during which I was working, and studying on my own. I believe with the right support, guidance, and professional context, that can be reduced substantially. I didn't have any formal education in Arts, Computers or VFX when I started this journey. I had a degree in Biology and 3 years of Architecture. If you have access to VFX courses in universities and VFX Studios where you can intern and possibly start your career at, then your path will be much straighter and shorter.

It is a very demanding role but also very rewarding and, in my opinion, the best platform to get to CG Supervisor.

A. **Building a Broad Skill Set**:
   - **Core Areas to Master**: To succeed as a generalist, focus on the primary areas of the VFX pipeline, such as 3D modeling, texturing, lighting, and compositing.
   - **Expanding Knowledge**: Generalists should be open to learning additional skills like basic rigging, animation, and even some scripting or tool creation if it benefits the project's needs.
B. **Learning Strategies for the Generalist Path:**
   - **Film Schools and Universities**: There are some amazing institutions providing degrees in VFX. In the following chapter, I list some of the best institutions for learning VFX, worldwide.
   - **Online Courses**: Platforms such as CGMA, Gnomon, and Rebelway provide access to courses covering a wide range of VFX topics. These courses usually include weekly homework assignments, live or recorded reviews of the student's

homework, a weekly live Q&A session, and direct communication access to the instructor, who will usually be an established professional in the VFX industry.

- **Pre-recorded Courses**: these will be very similar to the previous but won't include access to an instructor, which also means there are no weekly assignments. They are a more affordable option and usually more suitable for those who can't commit to follow the delivery schedule of the homework assignments or prefer to go through the content at their own pace. Patreon will also be a great source of quality paid content.
- **Online Tutorials**: YouTube and Vimeo are full of free content covering pretty much all VFX topics. These are not structured, and the quality varies a lot. Still, once you gather some experience watching online courses and tutorials it will become easier for you to identify the best sources and structure your own learning path. A bit of warning, this option might be the cheapest option, but it is also the hardest to bring to fruition in terms of actual learning and skill development. It requires extremely high levels of self-discipline and determination that are not commonly found in most people. For most people these sources of knowledge will be extremely valuable for filling some lacunae and for support on solving specific problems.
- **Personal Projects**: Practicing on a variety of projects will expose you to different workflows and problems, enhancing your skills in each area of the pipeline.
- **Collaborative Projects**: Working with other artists helps generalists understand how their work affects other departments and develop collaborative skills crucial in a studio environment.

C. **Balancing Depth and Breadth**:
- While it's essential to develop skills across disciplines, generalists should aim to reach a solid level of expertise in at least one or two core areas, such as modeling and texturing. This provides a foundation they can build on while expanding their other skills more broadly.

SOME SCHOOLS WILL BE BETTER THAN OTHERS

Here are five of the top schools and universities in Europe renowned for their Visual Effects (VFX) programs:

- *Gobelins, l'École de l'Image* (Paris, France)
  Gobelins is internationally acclaimed for its animation and VFX programs, offering comprehensive training that combines artistic and technical skills. It has consistently ranked as the top animation school in Europe.
- *Bournemouth University* (Bournemouth, United Kingdom)
  Through its National Centre for Computer Animation (NCCA), Bournemouth University provides specialized courses in computer animation and VFX, emphasizing both creative and technical aspects. It is recognized as one of the leading institutions for animation and VFX education in Europe.
- *The Animation Workshop/VIA University College* (Viborg, Denmark)
  This institution offers a Bachelor of Arts in Character Animation and a Bachelor of Arts in Computer Graphic Arts, both of which include VFX components. It is highly regarded for its focus on practical skills and industry collaboration.
- *ARTFX* (Montpellier, France)
  ARTFX specializes in training students in CGI, VFX, 3D Animation, 2D Animation, and Video Games. Established by industry professionals, it offers programs that are closely aligned with current industry standards and practices.
- *Escape Studios* (London, United Kingdom)
  Part of Pearson College London, Escape Studios offers undergraduate, postgraduate, and short courses in VFX, Animation, Games, and Motion Graphics. It is recognized for its industry-focused curriculum and strong ties with leading studios.

Here are five of the top schools and universities in the United States:

- *Gnomon School of Visual Effects* (Hollywood, California)
  Often referred to as the "MIT of visual effects," Gnomon offers specialized programs in VFX, including a Bachelor of Fine Arts in Digital Production and a Certificate in Digital Production for Entertainment. The school is known for its industry-focused curriculum and high placement rates.
- *Savannah College of Art and Design (SCAD)* (Savannah, Georgia)
  SCAD provides comprehensive VFX programs at the bachelor's and master's levels, emphasizing both technical skills and creative artistry. The college boasts state-of-the-art facilities and a strong track record of alumni working in major studios.
- *University of Southern California (USC)* (Los Angeles, California)
  USC's School of Cinematic Arts offers programs that integrate VFX with film and animation studies, providing students with a

broad understanding of the entertainment industry. Its location in Los Angeles offers students ample networking opportunities.

- *School of Visual Arts (SVA)* (New York, New York)
  SVA offers a Bachelor of Fine Arts in Computer Art, Computer Animation, and Visual Effects, focusing on both the artistic and technical aspects of VFX. The program is taught by industry professionals and emphasizes hands-on experience.
- *Academy of Art University* (San Francisco, California)
  The Academy offers VFX programs that cover a wide range of skills, from compositing to 3D animation. The curriculum is designed to mirror industry standards, preparing students for careers in film, television, and gaming.

And here are five renowned institutions outside Europe and the United States:

- *Vancouver Film School (VFS) – Vancouver, Canada*
  VFS offers a comprehensive 3D Animation & Visual Effects program that has produced alumni credited on top-grossing animated films worldwide. The curriculum covers all aspects of VFX production, from concept development to post-production.
- *3dsense Media School—Singapore*
  Recognized globally, 3dsense provides industry-based training in Visual Effects, Animation, Game Art, and Motion Design. Since 2015, it has consistently ranked among the top 10 art schools worldwide by The Rookies World School Rankings.
- *Media Design School—Auckland, New Zealand*
  As a member of Laureate International Universities, Media Design School offers degrees in 3D Animation & Visual Effects, among other digital arts disciplines. The institution is known for its strong industry connections and practical approach to education.
- *SF Film School—Seoul, South Korea*
  SF Film School is renowned for its specialized programs in VFX and 3D animation. Instructors have worked on notable films such as *Life of Pi* and *Deadpool*, providing students with industry-relevant skills and knowledge.
- *Beijing Film Academy—Beijing, China*
  As one of the most prestigious film schools in Asia, Beijing Film Academy offers programs that include VFX training. The academy has a strong focus on both the artistic and technical aspects of filmmaking, preparing students for various roles in the industry.

TECHNICAL PROFICIENCY, CREATIVITY, AND PROBLEM-SOLVING

A CG generalist's value lies in their technical proficiency across disciplines, their ability to creatively adapt, and their problem-solving skills. Striking a balance between technical and creative skills allows generalists to address a variety of tasks, adapting as needed to meet the project's demands.

A. **Technical Proficiency across Multiple Tools**:
   • **3D Modeling and Animation Software**: Proficiency in software like Houdini, Maya, Blender, and ZBrush is essential for modeling, animation, and effects work.

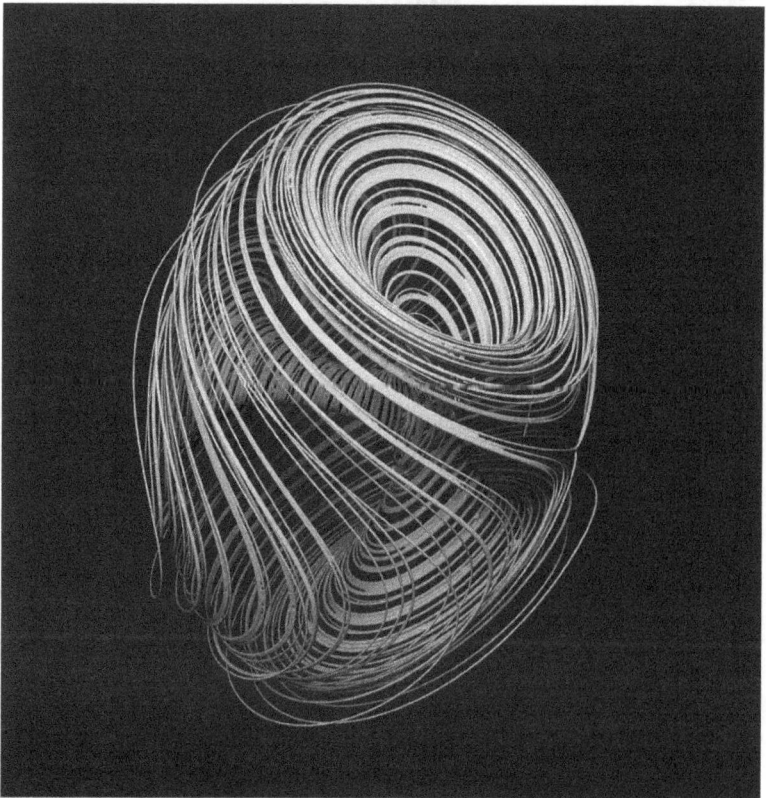

FIGURE 5.2 A personal project that illustrates the title of this chapter very well.

- **Texturing and Shading**: Generalists should be comfortable with tools like Substance Painter, Mari, and Photoshop to create textures and shaders that bring their models to life.
- **Lighting and Compositing**: Familiarity with lighting in rendering engines like Arnold, V-Ray, and Redshift, as well as compositing software like Nuke and Fusion, is necessary for producing cohesive final renders.

B. **Creativity and Adaptability:**
- Generalists must be highly adaptable, using creative problem-solving to address unexpected challenges. They often need to find efficient ways to complete tasks that meet the project's aesthetic and technical standards.
- Understanding design principles such as composition, color theory, and storytelling helps generalists make artistic decisions that enhance the quality of their work, regardless of the technical requirements.

C. **Problem-Solving and Efficiency**:
- In a fast-paced industry, generalists are often tasked with finding quick, practical solutions to meet tight deadlines or solve technical issues. Strong problem-solving skills enable them to assess project requirements and apply the most effective methods.
- **Tool-Building and Automation**: Some generalists may also dabble in scripting or tool development to streamline repetitive tasks, enhancing their productivity and workflow within a project.

THE PROS AND CONS

While a generalist's broad skill set can be valuable in the VFX industry, this path also presents unique challenges. Understanding the benefits and drawbacks of being a generalist will help you make informed decisions about whether this career path aligns with your goals and personality.

A. **Advantages of Being a Generalist**:
- **Versatility and Employability**: Generalists are adaptable, making them valuable assets in smaller studios, startups, or freelance roles where flexibility is required. Their broad skill set allows them to handle multiple tasks, increasing their employability across various project types.

- **Diverse Career Opportunities**: By having a wide range of skills, generalists are not limited to one type of role or project. They can transition between roles, adapt to new software, and take on different types of work, making them well-suited to dynamic and evolving projects.
- **Understanding of the Full Production Pipeline**: A generalist's broad knowledge of the VFX pipeline allows them to see the "big picture," making them valuable in roles that require a holistic understanding of how different departments interact.

B. **Challenges of the Generalist Path:**

- **Risk of Being "Jack of All Trades, Master of None"**: Without deep specialization, some generalists may struggle to stand out in areas that require high levels of expertise. This can be a disadvantage in larger studios, where specialists are typically valued for their in-depth knowledge.
- **Limited Advancement in Specialized Roles**: In larger studios or highly specialized projects, generalists may find it harder to advance due to the focus on specialized skills within specific departments.
- **High Learning Curve**: Generalists must keep up with multiple disciplines, tools, and workflows, which can be demanding and time intensive.

C. **Navigating the Generalist Path:**

- To thrive as a generalist, it's essential to be aware of the industry's demands. Seek roles that appreciate versatility and environments that encourage cross-disciplinary work.
- Consider balancing your skill set by building depth in one or two areas of the VFX pipeline while maintaining a broad understanding of others. This "T-shaped" skill profile provides both versatility and a foundation of expertise, giving you a unique edge.

Advancing to Senior and Lead Positions

6

As you gain experience and refine your skills in the VFX industry, the next step is often progressing to a senior position. These roles carry increased responsibility and require not only technical expertise but also leadership, strategic thinking, and the ability to mentor others. This section explores the path to senior and lead positions, offering insights into what it takes to succeed, build expertise, and foster a supportive professional network. From honing specialized skills to developing interpersonal skills, this guide will help you navigate the steps needed to advance in your VFX career.

SENIOR CG ARTIST ROLES AND RESPONSIBILITIES

A senior CG artist is an expert in their field with years of experience and a demonstrated ability to take on complex tasks. Senior artists are leaders within their departments, setting a high standard for quality and efficiency and often serving as mentors to junior team members.

A. **Defining the Role of a Senior CG Artist:**
- Senior CG artists are responsible for handling the most technically challenging and creative tasks within their specialization, whether that's animation, modeling, lighting, or compositing.
- They act as role models within their departments, showcasing a blend of technical precision and artistic sensibility, and

FIGURE 6.1 ZBrush Render of an elder man from my years of practicing sculpting skills.

they are often involved in decision-making for projects and workflows.

B. **Responsibilities and Expectations:**
- **Problem-Solving**: Often faced with complex technical challenges, senior artists are adept at troubleshooting and developing innovative solutions.
- **Quality Control**: Senior artists are responsible for ensuring that the work meets the highest standards. They review and refine their work and that of junior artists, ensuring consistency and quality across the project.
- **Mentorship and Training**: Senior artists are expected to help train junior team members, sharing their knowledge and guiding them through technical and artistic challenges.

C. **Leadership and Collaboration:**
- Senior artists work closely with department leads, supervisors, directors, and producers, providing feedback and insights that contribute to the overall vision of the project. They must communicate effectively across departments to ensure that their work aligns with the project's goals.

GAINING EXPERTISE IN SPECIALIZED AREAS

Moving into senior roles requires a deep understanding of specialized areas within the VFX pipeline. This expertise allows senior artists to tackle complex tasks with confidence and authority. Gaining specialized knowledge and continuously refining skills in a focused area can set you apart in the industry.

A. **Identifying Your Specialization**:
   - As you advance in your career, it's beneficial to identify specific areas within VFX that resonate with you, whether that's character modeling, advanced rigging, photorealistic lighting, or high-end FX simulations. Specializing in a particular niche can make you a go-to expert in that area.
   - **Research and Explore**: Stay informed about industry trends and emerging technologies within your specialization. Researching case studies, following industry leaders, and analyzing high-quality work in your field can give you valuable insights.

B. **Building Advanced Skills:**
   - **Technical Mastery**: Master the tools and techniques required for your chosen specialization. For instance, a senior FX artist would need deep expertise in Houdini for fluid and particle simulations, while a senior lighting artist might focus on advanced rendering techniques in Arnold or Vray.
   - **Artistic Excellence**: Strive to refine the artistic aspects of your specialization. For example, if you're focused on character animation, work on expressing emotion and movement with subtlety and nuance to elevate the quality of your work.
   - **Attention to Detail**: Senior artists are known for their meticulous attention to detail. Developing an eye for detail, whether in texture, motion, lighting, or compositing, is essential for producing work that meets the industry's highest standards.

C. **Keeping Skills Up to Date:**
   - The VFX industry evolves rapidly, and tools, techniques, and workflows are constantly improving. To stay relevant, senior artists should continuously learn and adapt, keeping up with new software features, plugins, and technologies that enhance their specialized skill set.

- **Attending Workshops and Industry Events**: Regularly attending conferences, workshops, and masterclasses can expose you to the latest advancements and best practices, as well as offer opportunities to network with other professionals.

NETWORKING AND MENTORING FOR CAREER GROWTH

Advancing to a senior role isn't only about technical skill; it's also about building strong professional relationships. Networking and mentoring play a

FIGURE 6.2 Personal Houdini creative exploration.

significant role in career growth, enabling you to learn from others, gain visibility in the industry, and contribute to the development of your team and peers.

A. **The Importance of Networking**:
  - **Building Connections**: Networking with colleagues, attending industry events, and joining online VFX communities are valuable ways to connect with other professionals. Building relationships within the industry can open doors to new opportunities, recommendations, and collaborations.
  - **Learning from Peers and Experts**: Networking allows you to exchange knowledge, insights, and experiences with others who may have different perspectives or areas of expertise. This can be particularly helpful when tackling new challenges or seeking inspiration for projects.
  - **Staying Informed**: Networking also helps you stay informed about industry trends, job openings, and potential career paths. Connecting with industry leaders and fellow artists can provide insights into new tools, techniques, and best practices. As well as giving you a better idea of what the near future looks like in terms of VFX projects planned or already shooting. This type of information can provide some guidance on what skills will be in high demand.

B. **Mentorship and Giving Back:**
  - **Being a Mentor**: As a senior artist, mentoring junior colleagues is an opportunity to give back and help shape the next generation of VFX professionals. Providing guidance and support to new artists not only benefits them but also strengthens your leadership and communication skills.
  - **Benefits of Mentorship**: Mentorship can be a mutually beneficial relationship, where both mentor and mentee learn and grow. Sharing knowledge often leads to new perspectives and fresh ideas, helping you refine your own skills and techniques.
  - **Fostering a Positive Work Culture**: By investing in mentoring, you contribute to a positive work environment, promoting a culture of collaboration and continuous learning within the studio.

C. **Professional Development through Networking and Mentorship:**
  - Actively participating in the VFX community—whether through online platforms, local meetups, or international conferences—reinforces your presence in the industry. This visibility can lead

to job offers, invitations to speak at events, or opportunities to collaborate on high-profile projects.

• **Joining Industry Organizations**: Organizations like SIGGRAPH, the Visual Effects Society (VES), and others provide resources and networking opportunities. Membership can enhance your credibility, connect you with professionals at various career stages, and offer platforms for sharing your work and insights.

Aspiring to be a CG Supervisor

7

Becoming a CG Supervisor is a significant milestone in the VFX industry. It represents not only a mastery of technical and artistic skills but also the development of leadership, communication, and management capabilities. This role serves as a bridge between the creative vision of the project and the technical execution by the team, requiring both strategic thinking and hands-on problem-solving. This section explores what it takes to transition from a senior artist to a CG Supervisor, the skills you'll need to succeed, and how to prepare for the leadership responsibilities that come with the role.

UNDERSTANDING THE CG SUPERVISOR ROLE

The CG Supervisor is at the heart of any VFX project, ensuring that the creative and technical aspects of the production are executed seamlessly. This chapter delves into the key responsibilities and challenges of this leadership position.

A. **Defining the CG Supervisor:**
  - A CG Supervisor is responsible for overseeing the entire CG production process, ensuring the technical and artistic quality of the work aligns with the project's vision.
  - They act as a critical point of communication between department leads, VFX Supervisors, and production teams, facilitating collaboration and troubleshooting issues.

B. **Responsibilities:**
- **Project Oversight**: Supervisors manage the CG pipeline, ensuring that assets are created, optimized, and integrated smoothly across departments.
- **Quality Assurance**: They are tasked with maintaining the artistic and technical standards of the project, reviewing work regularly and providing constructive feedback to team members.
- **Problem-Solving**: When technical or creative challenges arise, CG Supervisors must identify and implement effective solutions while keeping the project on track.
- **Team Leadership**: Supervisors guide teams of artists, fostering a positive and productive working environment while ensuring deadlines and milestones are met.

C. **Key Skills and Attributes:**
- **Technical Mastery**: A deep understanding of the entire CG pipeline, including modeling, animation, texturing, lighting, rendering, and compositing.
- **Leadership and Communication**: The ability to inspire and guide teams, mediate conflicts, and communicate clearly with both technical and non-technical stakeholders.
- **Adaptability**: The flexibility to pivot strategies when faced with unforeseen challenges or changes in the project scope.

TRANSITIONING FROM SENIOR ARTIST TO SUPERVISOR

The leap from senior artist to CG Supervisor involves more than just technical skills; it's a shift in mindset and responsibilities. This chapter provides a roadmap for making this transition successfully.

A. **Developing Leadership Skills**:
- **Mentorship as a Steppingstone**: Start by mentoring junior artists, offering guidance and feedback on their work. This experience helps build your leadership capabilities and establishes you as a go-to resource within your team.
- **Taking Initiative**: Proactively take on responsibilities that go beyond your current role, such as leading meetings, assisting in pipeline development, or solving cross-departmental challenges.

B. **Broadening Your Perspective:**
  - **Understanding the Entire Pipeline**: Supervisors need to see the big picture. Expand your knowledge of how other departments work and how your role interacts with theirs.
  - **Collaborating with Production Teams**: Engage with producers and project managers to understand scheduling, resource allocation, and budgeting—skills crucial for supervisory roles.

C. **Building Trust and Authority:**
  - As you take on more responsibilities, establish yourself as a dependable team member who can handle complex challenges and guide others effectively.
  - Demonstrating calmness under pressure and a collaborative attitude will help you earn the trust of your colleagues and supervisors.

D. **Preparing for the Transition:**
  - Seek feedback from supervisors and peers about your readiness for leadership roles. Use this input to identify areas for improvement and focus on developing those skills.
  - Take advantage of training opportunities, workshops, and online courses that focus on management and leadership in the VFX industry.

My personal experience of making this transition came a bit unexpectedly and without planning, though most of the previous points were already happening naturally.

I knew CG Supervisor would be one of the most likely career paths available for me, but I wasn't even sure I wanted to take on that role since it meant spending less time doing and a lot more time supervising and in meetings...

Truth is, when I got the invitation, I didn't hesitate to say yes. Looking back, I realize I wasn't fully aware of all the tasks and responsibilities that come with the job, and I think I said yes so promptly because I like to challenge myself and because I knew it was the acknowledgment of my dedication and capabilities. I also trusted the people inviting me to assume this role wouldn't ask me if they didn't think I was ready. I was very lucky to get such an amazing team to take me on my first CG Supervisor experience. Their planning gave me the opportunity to start on a smaller project to learn and grow in order to gradually assume the role in bigger productions.

Naturally I kept comparing me to those I recognize as amazing CG Supervisors. Trying to get their input, their advice... and I confess that for the first couple of years I felt a bit of fraud and not really at the same level. Not sure how natural that part was but I kept on going and giving my best, believing in myself, improving myself and eventually came a moment where I realized how comfortable I was in this role of CG Supervisor. It was also only at that same moment that I first became conscious of that "fraud" feeling. It was through its absence that its past presence became perceptible.

Psychology aside, it has been an amazing and extremely rewarding journey so far. I'm very glad I accepted this role and I'm very thankful to those who gave me this opportunity. Looking forward to seeing what comes next.

LEADERSHIP, COMMUNICATION, AND MANAGEMENT SKILLS

One of the most significant aspects of being a CG Supervisor is leading and managing teams effectively. This chapter focuses on the essential leadership, communication, and organizational skills needed to succeed in this role.

A. **Leadership in the VFX Industry**:
- **Inspiring Your Team**: A good supervisor motivates their team by fostering a sense of purpose and collaboration. Set clear goals and encourage creativity and innovation within your team.
- **Leading by Example**: Demonstrate professionalism, accountability, and a commitment to excellence. Your behavior sets the tone for your team's culture and work ethic.

FIGURE 7.1 Dreamcatchers Tribe—personal project.

B. **Effective Communication:**
- **Clear and Concise Communication**: Supervisors must convey complex ideas to diverse teams, including artists, technical staff, and production leads. Clarity and adaptability in your communication style are essential.
- **Providing Feedback**: Constructive feedback is a critical part of leadership. Learn to deliver feedback that is specific, actionable, and encouraging to help team members grow and improve.
- **Listening Skills**: Being an effective listener is just as important as communicating your own ideas. Understand the concerns and suggestions of your team to build a collaborative environment.

C. **Management Skills:**
- **Time and Resource Management**: Supervisors are responsible for ensuring that projects stay on schedule and within budget. This requires careful planning and prioritization of tasks.
- **Conflict Resolution**: Inevitably, conflicts may arise within the team or between departments. Supervisors must mediate these conflicts effectively, ensuring that the team remains focused and cohesive.
- **Performance Monitoring**: Regularly assess the progress and performance of team members. Recognize achievements, address areas for improvement, and ensure that everyone is aligned with the project's objectives.

D. **Continuous Self-improvement:**
- Leadership is a skill that requires ongoing refinement. Seek out mentorship, attend leadership seminars, and reflect on your own experiences to continue growing in your role.
- Stay adaptable and open to new ideas, technologies, and approaches that can enhance your effectiveness as a supervisor.

The Creative and Technical Aspects of CG Supervision

8

CG Supervision is where artistry and engineering meet. At this level, supervisors must not only understand the intricacies of the VFX pipeline but also balance creative vision with technical execution across departments and deliverables. They are problem solvers, team leaders, and quality gatekeepers. In this section, we explore the core creative and technical responsibilities of a CG Supervisor and how they ensure both visual excellence and production efficiency.

PROJECT MANAGEMENT AND SUPERVISION

At its core, the role of a CG Supervisor is about managing people, processes, and pixels. They keep the creative vision intact while ensuring the project stays within time and budget constraints.

A. **Setting the Creative and Technical Direction:**
   - CG Supervisors interpret the overall vision of the VFX or film director into actionable plans for the CG team.
   - They define the technical approach and quality standards expected.
   - This often includes approving look development, defining lighting templates, or setting shader libraries that will be reused across the show.

DOI: 10.1201/9781003494485-8

B. **Managing Schedules, Teams, and Milestones:**
- Working closely with production managers and VFX producers, the supervisor breaks down tasks into milestones and tracks progress.
- They help production allocate resources, adjust schedules as challenges arise, and ensure each artist understands its priorities.
- A strong supervisor understands team dynamics—knowing who needs support, who can be autonomous, and how to keep motivation high.

C. **Reviews and Feedback Loops:**
- Supervisors lead dailies and review sessions where artists present work for feedback.
- They must give clear, constructive notes that are both creatively insightful and technically actionable.
- Managing morale is crucial here; feedback should drive quality without demoralizing the team.

D. **Pipeline and Workflow Oversight:**
- A CG Supervisor often collaborates with pipeline TDs to design workflows that optimize render times, reduce redundancies, and ensure smooth data handoff across departments.
- If the pipeline breaks, they're often the first person called to help resolve or escalate the issue.

PROBLEM-SOLVING IN VFX

No VFX project goes off without a hitch. Whether it's a broken rig, a misaligned render pass, or a director's last-minute creative change, CG Supervisors must be master problem-solvers.

A. **Diagnosing Technical Bottlenecks:**
- Supervisors need enough technical depth to troubleshoot issues across departments—be it a buggy simulation, render failures, or assets that don't meet the brief.
- They work closely with department leads and TDs to track down root causes and implement fixes without derailing the schedule.

B. **Creative Problem-Solving under Pressure:**
- Directors may change their mind mid-shot or push for more ambitious visuals late in production.

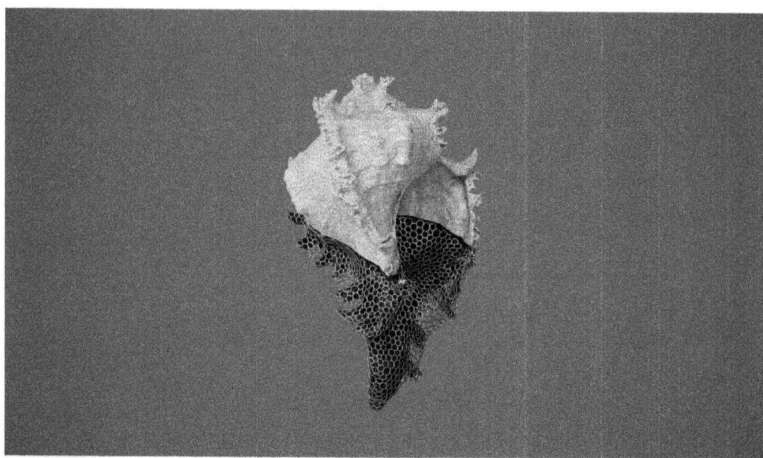

FIGURE 8.1   An image that came from the need to solve a problem—personal project.

- It's up to the CG Supervisor to evaluate whether the request is feasible and, if so, how to pivot the team with minimal disruption.

C. **Prioritization and Risk Assessment:**
  - Supervisors constantly weigh the cost of "perfect" versus "good enough."
  - Sometimes a small compromise on visual fidelity in the background can free up time for hero shots. These trade-offs are daily decisions.

D. **Empowering Team-Based Solutions**
  - Rather than solving everything solo, strong supervisors foster a culture of ownership.
  - They encourage artists and leads to bring their own solutions to the table, creating a sense of investment and innovation.

COLLABORATING WITH OTHER DEPARTMENTS

A CG Supervisor doesn't work in a vacuum. Their effectiveness depends on how well they collaborate across all VFX and production departments.

A. **Interfacing with the VFX Supervisor and Director**:
  - The CG Supervisor is often the "translator" between the VFX Supervisor's creative brief and the CG team's execution.
  - They ensure technical solutions meet the artistic vision, flag concerns early, and help manage client or director expectations.
B. **Working with Production and Editorial:**
  - CG Supervisors must understand the post-production timeline and delivery specifications.
  - They coordinate with the editorial team on turnovers, plate updates, and final handoffs to ensure accurate integration and timing.
C. **Communication as a Leadership Tool**
  - Great supervisors tailor their communication style to the audience—technical with TDs, visionary with directors, empathetic with artists.
  - They listen actively, de-escalate conflicts, and keep communication lines open so no one feels isolated or out of sync.

Final Thoughts on Creative and Technical Leadership

A Supervisor position in VFX is as much about people as pixels. It's about knowing when to push, when to support, and when to innovate. By mastering the balance between creativity and structure, VFX Supervisors lead teams to deliver not just finished shots—but exceptional visual storytelling. CG Supervisors will have a similar role within their 3D department, so the same people and communication skills are valued. While the CG Supervisor takes on a leading role to its team, he also has to be able to interpret and follow the VFX Supervisor's instructions. Most of the times presenting solutions, sometimes raising problems and occasionally defending an idea that goes in a different direction.

The Next Step—VFX Supervisor

9

For many CG artists and supervisors, the role of VFX Supervisor represents the pinnacle of creative and technical leadership. It's a role that combines deep pipeline knowledge, aesthetic vision, team leadership, and production strategy. VFX Supervisors are responsible for the final look and integration of all visual effects across a project—balancing artistic goals with practical realities and often working directly with directors and producers to bring visual stories to life.

In this section, we explore what it means to become a VFX Supervisor, the skills and mindset needed to thrive in the role, and how to navigate the transition from CG supervision to leading entire VFX projects from concept to delivery.

EXPLORING THE ROLE OF THE VFX SUPERVISOR

The VFX Supervisor sits at the intersection of art, technology, storytelling, and production. This chapter breaks down what the job truly entails and what makes it one of the most demanding—and rewarding—roles in the industry.

A. **Scope and Responsibility:**
   - The VFX Supervisor is ultimately responsible for the quality, consistency, and feasibility of all visual effects in a given project.
   - They supervise the work of every VFX department, from previs and asset creation to compositing and final delivery, ensuring the output meets the director's vision and the production's technical needs.

DOI: 10.1201/9781003494485-9

B. **Creative Collaboration with the Director**
   - The supervisor acts as a key liaison between the VFX studio and the film or series director, helping translate abstract ideas into visual language.
   - They provide creative solutions during pre-production, offer on-set guidance during principal photography, and lead the post-production VFX team in realizing the final look.

C. **Strategic Leadership**
   - A VFX Supervisor must plan ahead. They work with producers and coordinators to create achievable schedules, estimate budgets, and design workflows that keep the show on track.
   - They must anticipate challenges, make fast decisions, and guide the team toward high-quality solutions with limited resources.

D. **Technical Authority**
   - Supervisors must have a broad and deep understanding of the VFX pipeline—from asset workflows to rendering, simulation, and real-time technologies.
   - They are expected to understand what's possible and how to do it efficiently. Whether troubleshooting render issues or defining a look-dev workflow, they are the technical anchor of the show.

TRANSITIONING FROM CG SUPERVISOR TO VFX SUPERVISOR

Becoming a VFX Supervisor is not just a promotion—it's a professional shift that demands a broader perspective, stronger communication, and more decisive leadership.

A. **Broadening beyond CG**
   - As a CG Supervisor, your domain likely focused on 3D assets and workflows. To make the leap, you need a working knowledge of all departments: compositing, layout, camera tracking, rotoscoping, and more.
   - Begin expanding your familiarity with 2D workflows, on-set supervision, and final shot delivery to develop a full-picture understanding of the VFX process.

B. **On-Set Experience**
   - One of the biggest shifts is working in live-action production environments. VFX Supervisors are often present during

shoots, advising on green screen setups, camera tracking markers, and lighting references.
- Gaining experience on set is essential—shadowing an experienced supervisor, contributing to shoot planning, or supervising smaller shoots is a great way to build this skill set.

C. **Leading across Departments and Studios**
- Unlike CG Supervisors who often lead a single department, VFX Supervisors can manage entire project teams even across multiple vendors or locations.
- This requires clear communication, diplomacy, and the ability to synthesize feedback from multiple creative voices (directors, production designers, editors) into a unified VFX vision.

D. **Managing Clients and Expectations**
- A major part of the role is managing the expectations of the client—be it a studio, network, or director.
- You must be able to present work-in-progress confidently, justify creative decisions, and diplomatically negotiate changes in scope, budget, or schedule.

MASTERING LEADERSHIP, VISION, AND EXECUTION

At the top level, being a VFX Supervisor is about leading a team and a vision with clarity, consistency, and inspiration. This chapter explores how to do that effectively.

A. **Vision and Consistency**
- You are the keeper of the visual integrity of the VFX. From early concept art through final comp, it's your responsibility to ensure a cohesive look and feel across the entire show.
- This requires an eye for detail, a strong understanding of storytelling, and the ability to guide look development early in the process.

B. **Communication and Team Motivation**
- Great VFX Supervisors know how to motivate a team. They balance high standards with empathy, give clear notes without micromanaging, and help their artists do their best work.
- Daily check-ins, dailies, and cross-team syncs are your tools—not just for quality control but for building morale and momentum.

C. **Problem-Solving and Crisis Management**
  - No project is without setbacks—failed simulations, misaligned approvals, shot cuts, or tight deadlines.
  - As a supervisor, you must remain calm under pressure, find creative workarounds, and keep production moving. Your confidence becomes the team's confidence.

D. **Legacy and Mentorship**
  - A great supervisor doesn't just deliver great work—they elevate others. By mentoring up-and-coming leads, advocating for your team, and fostering a collaborative studio culture, you build a legacy that lasts beyond the project.
  - Your leadership can shape not just visuals, but careers.

Final Thoughts: The Next Evolution of Your Career

The role of the VFX Supervisor is demanding, complex, and deeply rewarding. It's where your skills as an artist, technician, leader, and collaborator converge. If you're drawn to big-picture thinking, cross-department collaboration, and guiding projects from vision to final pixels, then this role may be your natural next step. The VFX industry is always evolving—and VFX Supervisors are among the people shaping its future.

Career Progression beyond CG Supervisor

10

Reaching the role of CG Supervisor or even VFX Supervisor is a major milestone in a visual effects career—but it's not the end of the road. For many professionals, this is where new opportunities begin to emerge: creative leadership, studio management, entrepreneurship, and executive positions. This section explores what lies beyond supervision and how experienced VFX professionals can shape their next chapter—whether they seek greater creative influence, business leadership, or a balance between the two.

EXPLORING EXECUTIVE AND CREATIVE LEADERSHIP ROLES

As your experience deepens and your leadership reputation grows, you may find yourself drawn toward high-level roles that impact not just projects—but the entire direction of a studio or brand. These roles blend creative vision with organizational influence.

A. Creative Director
- Creative Directors guide the artistic voice across multiple projects, departments, or even an entire studio brand.
- Unlike VFX Supervisors who focus on a specific project, Creative Directors influence pitches, aesthetics, and client relationships on a broader scale.

DOI: 10.1201/9781003494485-10

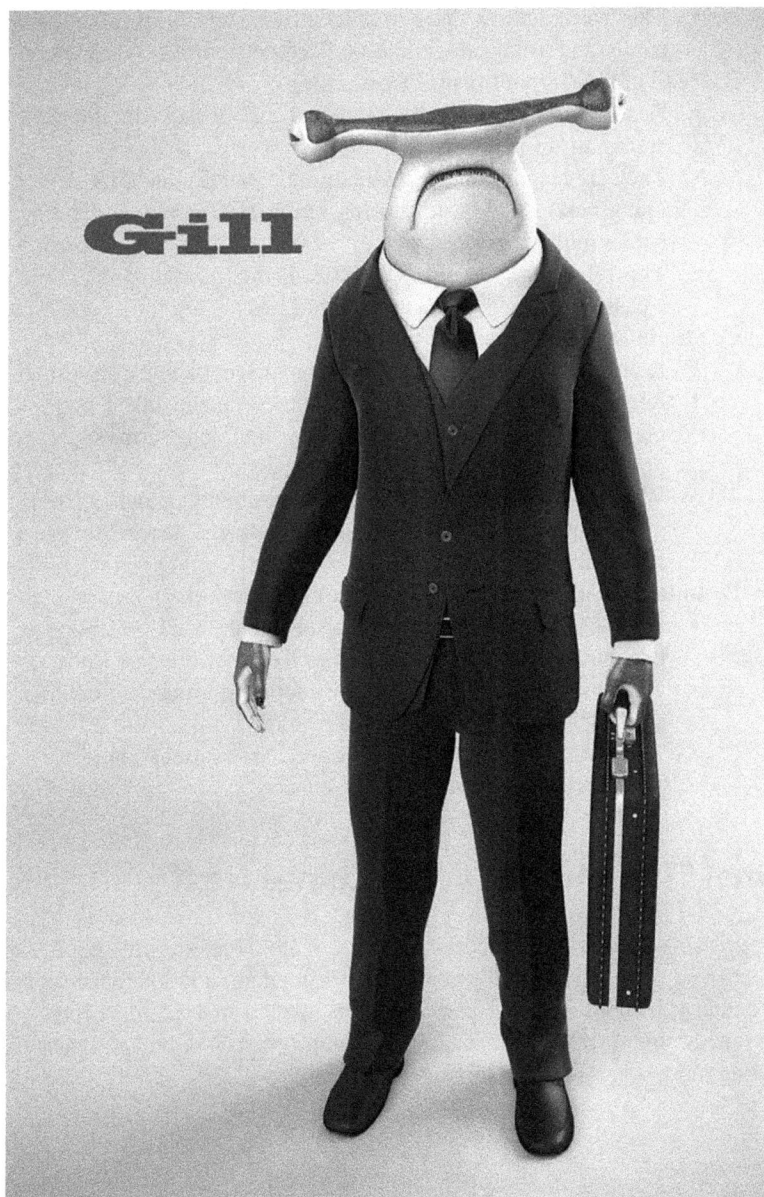

FIGURE 10.1 Character from a personal project.

- This role requires deep artistic insight, an ability to inspire teams, and strong presentation skills for clients and stakeholders.

B. **Head of CG/Departmental Leadership**
- Heads of CG oversee the technical and artistic development across an entire department.
- They are responsible for maintaining pipeline standards, developing best practices, mentoring senior staff, and coordinating across multiple projects.
- This role suits supervisors with strong organizational skills and a passion for long-term growth strategies.

C. **Studio Director/Head of Studio**
- At the highest level, studio directors manage the entire operation.
- Responsibilities include business development, talent recruitment, client acquisition, budgeting, and long-term strategic planning.
- While still rooted in creativity, this position demands a strong understanding of business fundamentals and leadership on a macro-level.

D. **Independent Consultant/Fractional Leadership**
- For those looking for variety, some experienced professionals become independent consultants or freelance creative leaders.
- They may advise on pipeline development, creative direction, studio structuring, or production workflows.
- This path allows more flexibility and the chance to contribute to a wider range of teams and challenges.

Final Thoughts on What Comes Next

Progressing beyond VFX Supervisor is a leap into the unknown—but it's also where you gain the most influence, creative freedom, and long-term impact. Whether you choose to guide projects, shape talent, run a studio, or forge your own path, this stage is about leading with purpose. You're no longer just executing the vision. You're defining it.

Essential Resources and Practices

11

Success in the VFX industry requires more than artistic talent and technical knowledge—it also depends on how well you manage your time, stay current with emerging trends, and continue investing in your professional growth. Whether you're just starting out or have years of experience, mastering the right habits and using the right tools can elevate your career and keep you moving forward in a competitive, fast-changing industry.

This section highlights the most valuable resources and best practices that every VFX professional should incorporate into their workflow and career development plan.

INDUSTRY CONFERENCES, WORKSHOPS, AND TRAINING

The VFX world evolves rapidly and staying relevant means embracing lifelong learning. Engaging with industry events and training resources gives you access to cutting-edge knowledge, creative inspiration, and invaluable networking opportunities.

- **Conferences and Trade Shows**
  - **SIGGRAPH:** One of the most important conferences in computer graphics, offering presentations, panels, and demos on the latest VFX innovations.
  - **FMX:** A European conference that blends technical deep dives with storytelling, production insights, and real-world case studies.

DOI: 10.1201/9781003494485-11

- **VIEW Conference, GDC (Game Developers Conference)**, and **Annecy Festival** also feature high-quality talks relevant to VFX artists working in games, film, and animation.
- **Workshops and Masterclasses**
  - Online platforms such as **CGMA, Rebelway, FXPHD, Gnomon, School of Motion**, and **Learn Squared** offer instructor-led, project-based courses from industry veterans.
  - Short-term bootcamps and live workshops often focus on high-demand topics such as Houdini FX, real-time workflows, or advanced compositing.
- **Studio-Initiated Training Programs**
  - Many larger studios offer in-house training and mentorship programs. Getting involved can help you gain access to tools, techniques, and workflows specific to that studio's pipeline.
  - Be proactive—ask about available programs, request shadowing opportunities, or propose study groups if one doesn't already exist.
- **Continuous Learning as a Career Strategy**
  - Staying up to date with new techniques (e.g., machine learning in rotoscoping, real-time rendering, or USD workflows) can make you a go-to resource on your team.
  - Prioritize depth in your area of focus, but don't neglect the value of cross-disciplinary knowledge—it builds versatility.

EFFECTIVE TIME AND PROJECT MANAGEMENT

Beyond technical skills, the ability to manage your workload efficiently is one of the most important—and underrated—qualities of a successful VFX professional.

A. **Personal Productivity Systems**
  - Use tools like **Notion, Trello**, or **Todoist** to manage daily tasks and keep long-term goals visible. Often the studios will already have those or similar tools available as part of a suite package deal with software providers.
  - Break down complex projects into smaller, manageable goals and celebrate each milestone.

B. **Studio Workflow and Pipeline Awareness**
- Understand how your work fits into the larger VFX pipeline. Stay aligned with department schedules, file naming conventions, version control, and delivery protocols.
- Communicate proactively—if you're blocked or falling behind, flag it early. Teams run smoother when challenges are shared early.

C. **Handling Tight Deadlines and Crunch**
- Time management isn't just about hitting deadlines—it's also about sustaining yourself during crunch periods.
- Build in recovery time, set boundaries when possible, and advocate for realistic timelines, especially if you're in a lead or supervisor role.

D. **Tools for Remote and Hybrid Teams**
- The rise of distributed production makes it essential to master collaborative tools like **Slack**, **ShotGrid**, **SyncSketch**, and cloud-based render management systems.
- Organize your files, document your process, and communicate clearly—especially when working asynchronously.

STAYING UPDATED ON VFX TRENDS AND TECHNOLOGY

The VFX industry is constantly evolving. Tools, techniques, and even entire pipelines change rapidly. Staying informed isn't optional—it's essential for your long-term relevance and success.

A. **Follow Key Sources**
- **Websites:** fxguide, ArtStation Magazine, 80.lv, and VFX Voice provide insight into tools, trends, and interviews with professionals.
- **YouTube Channels and Podcasts:** Channels like Corridor Crew, Ian Hubert, and CG Geek offer both entertainment and education. Podcasts like "The VFX Show" or "CG Garage" provide in-depth industry discussion.

B. **Understand Where the Industry Is Headed**
- **Real-Time and Virtual Production**: With the rise of Unreal Engine and LED volumes, real-time workflows are changing how studios approach VFX.

- **AI and Machine Learning**: From rotoscoping to denoising and crowd simulations, AI is becoming increasingly integrated into production pipelines.
- **Cloud Collaboration and Render Farms**: As cloud-based pipelines mature, artists can collaborate globally and render high-quality shots without on-premises infrastructure.

C. **Participate in Community and Knowledge Sharing**
- Join forums like **r/vfx**, **CGSociety**, and Discord communities dedicated to specific tools or disciplines.
- Share your work, ask for feedback, and contribute where you can. Active participation makes you more visible and can lead to unexpected opportunities.

D. **Build Time for Exploration**
- Reserve time each week—or even monthly—to experiment with a new tool, software update, or creative technique.
- Don't wait for a production need to learn something new. Staying ahead gives you a competitive edge.

Final Thoughts: Sharpening Your Tools for the Long Game

It's not enough to master your craft once—you have to keep refining it. The most successful VFX professionals view learning and optimization as part of their daily practice. By investing in the right resources, managing your time effectively, and staying plugged into the pulse of the industry, you'll not only stay relevant—you'll stay inspired.

Real-World Insights and Success Stories

12

The VFX industry is built not just on tools and techniques, but on people—each with a unique path, shaped by personal goals, unexpected turns, and a constantly evolving creative landscape. This section goes beyond the workflow and into the lived experience of working in VFX: the pivotal lessons, the long-term perspective, and the mindset needed to survive—and thrive—through both stability and chaos.

The stories and reflections shared in this section aim to ground the theory presented in the rest of the book, offering clarity and confidence to those navigating their own VFX career.

INTERVIEWS WITH VFX PROFESSIONALS

My path and experience may seem very peculiar but there are many interesting real-life stories of people succeeding in the VFX industry. To illustrate this, I asked a few colleagues who were kind enough to help me with this book, the same six questions. In this chapter, I do a brief presentation of who they are, and I share their answers. This is in my opinion one of the most valuable contents of the book.

Timo Hanczuk—Compositing Supervisor

Born in 1992

DOI: 10.1201/9781003494485-12

FIGURE 12.1 Photo of Timo.

1. What is your current position and how long have you had the job?

   Timo: I am currently a Compositing Supervisor and I'm holding that position since 4 years.

2. What was your career path to get to your current position? How did you start and what other positions did you have along the way?

   Timo: I began my career with a 6-month internship at Pixomondo before pursuing a degree in Audiovisual Media at the Hochschule der Medien Stuttgart. I then completed another internship at Mackevision, where I later wrote my Bachelor Thesis and continued working after graduation. Mackevision eventually became Accenture Song VFX, and after a few years, I was given the opportunity to work on a project as a lead compositor. As part of that role, I also stepped in for the Compositing Supervisor during his absence. This gradually introduced me to the tasks and responsibilities of the position, ultimately leading to my promotion for the next project.

3. What is your educational background?

Timo: I earned a Bachelor's degree in Audiovisual Media from the Hochschule der Medien in Stuttgart. The program covered a wide range of audiovisual media, including film, television, radio and interactive media, with a small focus on visual effects. Although the visual effects portion was limited, the broad knowledge I gained has been invaluable, especially when different departments overlap and in understanding on-set and in-camera processes. Additionally, the visual effects industry in Stuttgart is relatively small, so building a network during my studies was crucial and ultimately led to my internship at Mackevision.

4. How would you describe your current position? Most common tasks, main responsibilities and main challenges

Timo: As a Compositing Supervisor my primary responsibility is overseeing the compositing process from start to finish. My most common tasks include reviewing shots and providing feedback to the compositing artists, troubleshooting technical issues and coordinating with the other departments to ensure a smooth production pipeline. One of the biggest challenges is balancing the creative vision and artistic quality with the technical constraints and the time pressure that often comes with the projects.

5. Are you happy at your current position or are you aiming for a different role?

Timo: I'm happy in my current position as Compositing Supervisor, but I also love working on shots as an artist. After completing bigger projects, I enjoy shifting back to a more hands-on role, which helps me stay connected to the creative process and continue improving my skills.

6. What advice would you give to a student or a junior artist aiming for your job?

Timo: My advice to a junior would be to focus on building a strong foundation in compositing skills. Take on diverse projects to broaden your skill set and seek mentorship from experienced artists. Always challenge yourself, while full CG shots are exciting, being skilled in handling difficult live-action plates is crucial. Also, be a supportive team member. Helping others and maintaining a positive reputation can be as important as your showreel for leadership opportunities. Finally, and most importantly, find the role that brings you the most joy. If you love working on shots, you should focus on that. But if you also enjoy guiding a team and manage projects, a supervisor role might be something you want to aim for.

Martin Lapp—Head of FX

Born in August 1988

1. What is your current position and how long have you had the job?

    Martin: I'm currently Head of FX at Accenture Song VFX and have been there since 5 months now.

2. What was your career path to get to your current position? How did you start and what other positions did you have along the way?

    Martin: I started as a freelance generalist for a long time. During my studies, I also worked as a CG Generalist at Method Studios in LA for 8 months. After I finished my Diploma, I started as a Junior FX TD at Trixter in Munich, Germany. Shortly after I moved to Vancouver, Canada where I continued as a Junior FX TD. I spent 3 years there and got promoted to mid, senior and Lead FX TD relatively quickly.

    I then moved back to Munich, Germany when the pandemic hit as FX Lead and became FX Supervisor there shortly after. For the last 3 years I was Head of FX there before joining Accenture Song VFX.

3. What is your educational background?

    Martin: After high school, I studied Film & Arts in Stuttgart for about a year. I then moved to Ludwigsburg to study Visual Effects at the Institute of Animation at Filmakademie Baden-Württemberg, Germany.

    I can highly recommend to not only study Animation of Visual Effects but also have a general Film education, which is a requirement after Filmakademie for the first 2 years.

4. How would you describe your current position? Most common tasks, main responsibilities and main challenges

    Martin: As Head of Department, I'm responsible for everything related to the FX Department and together with Pipeline, ensuring the most efficient way of working with other departments as well. On a show, I mostly spend time in FX rounds or VFX Dailies together with the other Heads and Supes. I mostly step in if there are issues on a show, where the FX Lead of Supervisor faces challenges that need additional support. Other than that, I jump in as FX Supervisor as well for certain

FIGURE 12.2 Photo of Martin.

Shows or do shot work whenever needed. Recently there is a lot of great collaboration with the Pipeline Team as well as we are building the USD Pipeline at Accenture and define department workflows.

5. Are you happy at your current position or are you aiming for a different role?

Martin: I am currently very happy in my current position but also always up for new challenges

6. What advice would you give to a student or a junior artist aiming for your job?

Martin: First of all, you really need to love what you're doing in VFX in general. There will be lots of compromises for your personal life and working hours can be tough sometimes. Making your hobby your Job in this case really goes a long way.

For FX in particular, I think it's important to have a well-balanced technical and artistic skillset as well as a certain pragmatic view on things as often times Houdini artists like to overcomplicate things, get lost in details or are in search for the next problem to solve, rather than finding the solution in the first place. And although FX is in part quite a specialized department, a background as a generalist definitely helps as well. After my Diploma, the only thing I really hadn't done yet was serious FX in Houdini. So, I decided to pursue that. Having a rock-solid understanding of all other departments, helped me climb up the ladder quite quickly.

David Anastácio—CG Supervisor

1. What is your current position and how long have you had the job?

David: I'm a CG Supervisor at Accenture Song #VFX (previously known as Mackevision), since 2019.

2. What was your career path to get to your current position? How did you start and what other positions did you have along the way?

David: My journey to becoming a CG Supervisor began in Portugal, where I started as a 3D generalist working mostly on commercial projects. During this time, I developed a broad range of skills, including animation, modeling, texturing, shading, rendering, editing, motion graphics, and camera work. The Compositing Supervisor during his absence. This gradually introduced me to the tasks and responsibilities of the position, ultimately leading to my promotion for the next project.

Choosing the stability of fixed contracts over freelancing, I didn't move between studios as frequently. However, I gradually transitioned to larger-scale commercial projects, films, and series, working at Pixomondo, Arri VFX, and Mackevision, continuing my work as a 3D generalist.

In 2015, I joined Mackevision as a Senior 3D Artist and, by 2017, advanced to Lead 3D Artist. Over time, my role expanded with increasing responsibilities and a growing team of artists to manage. This natural progression led to my first official project as a CG Supervisor for Netflix's Lost in Space.

3. What is your educational background?

David: I started university in 2003 at the Fine Arts Academy of Lisbon University, with no plans to pursue 3D or VFX. My focus was on Industrial Design. It wasn't until my 3rd year that I discovered 3D, getting introduced to SolidWorks, Cinema 4D R9, and 3Ds Max 7 as tools to develop designs and refine ideas faster. Eventually this new area of interest grew more and more and became my main focus by year 4 of university, this was all as a side project, as we didn't have any computer classes back in the day, so I had to learn by myself and read a lot of books.

As I began my 5th year of university, I received a job offer to work full-time at a small 3D studio in Lisbon. I jumped at the opportunity, as it was a significant step up from balancing my studies with weekend work. As a result, my final year of university was mostly spent working as a 3D artist, attending classes primarily to present projects and take exams.

4. How would you describe your current position? Most common tasks, main responsibilities and main challenges

David: As a CG Supervisor, I oversee a team of 3D artists, primarily generalists, providing feedback, solving technical challenges, and creating 3D setups and tools to support their work. In addition to the creative side, I'm involved in management and production tasks such as project biddings, scheduling, team coordination, and client communication. The biggest challenge is the daily problem-solving, but that's also what I enjoy most about VFX—every day brings a new puzzle to solve.

5. Are you happy at your current position or are you aiming for a different role?

David: I'm very happy with my current role, as 3D is my passion, and being a CG Supervisor allows me to stay hands-on with it. There's no higher position that would let me continue working directly in 3D. In this role, I get to support artists and tackle challenges daily which is exactly what I enjoy most.

6. What advice would you give to a student or a junior artist aiming for your job?

David: As a supervisor, a major part of the job is helping artists solve problems and providing artistic feedback, which requires a strong blend of artistic ability, technical expertise, problem-solving skills, and soft skills—since much of the role involves communication. While all these skills are essential, if I had to prioritize one, it would be a strong artistic sense and a keen critical eye. After all, the ultimate goal is to create visually captivating images.

Emanuel Fuchs—VFX Supervisor

Born in October 1989

1. What is your current position and how long have you had the job?
    Emanuel: I'm a Visual Effects Supervisor at Accenture Song, and I've been working in that capacity since 2019.

FIGURE 12.3   Photo of Emanuel.

2. What was your career path to get to your current position? How did you start and what other positions did you have along the way?
3. What is your educational background?

   Emanuel: Back when I was 13, I came across modding for games—starting with simple scripting changes, then visual changes like textures, and eventually diving into 3D. There were some tutorials out there, so I kept learning as much as I possibly could and soon became part of a larger total conversion mod team.

I stuck with that for a while until the limitations of the game engine at the time (2048 vertices per creature, for example...) became too restrictive for the creative visions I wanted to realize. So, I shifted my focus toward VFX. I bought a camcorder and watched tutorials on matchmoving so I could integrate my renders into footage—without limitations. Well... except for the non-existent render farm, which became the next limitation, haha.

All of this happened while I was still in school. Since I loved doing 3D and VFX so much, I started looking into universities to follow that path professionally after graduating. My research showed that Filmakademie Ludwigsburg was one of the best options in Germany. However, they required at least 1 year of professional experience before even accepting applications. So, I did a 1 year internship at a small studio near Stuttgart.

After that, I managed to get a spot at the Filmakademie and studied Film and Media with a focus on VFX.

With my 3rd-year project, I won the Student VES Award and landed a job at Method Studios Los Angeles as a CG Artist. So, I relocated to the States and expanded my generalist skill set with Houdini (I started with Max, did a lot of Maya after that, until I finally picked the right package :D).

After gaining a lot of experience, I returned to Germany. While I was still finishing my studies, Mackevision (now Accenture Song) needed CG reinforcement and offered me a contract right away.

I joined them in mid-2016 as a 3D Artist but have worked in a variety of roles ever since.

For example: I worked on crowds for Game of Thrones, previs/techvis and shoot prep for Jim Button 1, FX work like combustion simulations for Porsche commercials, and on-set visualization using Ncam for Disney's The Nutcracker.

In 2018, a good friend of mine—who is a commercial director—approached me to help with his latest project, which involved a lot of VFX. Mackevision had capacity at the time, so we wanted to do it.

The "catch"? He wanted me to take on a leading role and be his main point of contact—otherwise, the project would've gone elsewhere. So, that became my first supervision role, including on-set supervision in Chicago.

More commercials followed, and eventually, my first TV show landed on my desk—HBO's Watchmen. Initially, I was responsible for the creature asset, but the main supervisor at our company was pulled into another project that grew much larger. So, he had to shift focus, and I stepped up to supervise Watchmen in 2019.

(Which is also when I got to know the author of this book)

4. How would you describe your current position? Most common tasks, main responsibilities and main challenges

Emanuel: First and foremost, I'm the connection between the client and our team. I try to figure out what the client wants—or work with them to develop ideas—and then pass those along to the team. Internally, I help brainstorm solutions to the client's problems, ensuring we find the most visually appealing and efficient way to approach them, and then present those solutions back to the client.

I'm also responsible for bidding and planning projects together with our producers. Depending on the size of the show, I sometimes even get the chance to do some hands-on work myself.

Beyond daily operations, I'm the main point of contact for the projects when it comes to interviews and presentations.

5. Are you happy at your current position or are you aiming for a different role?

Emanuel: I'm pretty happy in my current role and enjoy the privilege of working with so many talented people. Of course, I sometimes wish I had more time to work on shots myself—after all, that's what got me into this industry in the first place—but having creative influence throughout the whole process definitely makes up for it.

6. What advice would you give to a student or a junior artist aiming for your job?

Emanuel: That's a tricky one! My advice would be: do what you love, try to become the best you can at it, and if things go well, you'll eventually be offered your first leadership roles.

When that happens, you really need to listen to yourself:

Do you enjoy this new type of work, or would you rather keep honing your craft as the best FX/CG/Comp/etc., artist you can be?

Both paths are valid, and both are needed.

You can force things for short-term gains, but if you let your passion guide you, it'll lead you down a much more sustainable and fulfilling path.

Rouven Dombrowski—Onset and Virtual Production Supervisor

1. What is your current position and how long have you had the job?

    Rouven: I'm the Onset and Virtual Production Supervisor of Accenture Song VFX. I'm working at Accenture/Mackevision in different positions for more than 17 years now.

2. What was your career path to get to your current position? How did you start and what other positions did you have along the way?

    Rouven: Everything started at the end of the 80's when the first Commodore home-computers arrived in our children's world. After being infected with the computer virus, I never got away from it.

Later, after leaving university I worked for 1 year for a small film production. I was working there as a generalist for editing, filming, 3D, 2D, etc. I moved to Stuttgart at the end of 2007 to work for Mackevision as a 3D Artist. At this time Mackevision was primarily working in the visualization business for the automotive industry. I started as a modeling artist, moved to the lighting & shading department and after some time I was working as a 3D/CG Supervisor.

Around 2010 the company was getting bigger, and I was also working as an Onset Supervisor for moving and still images. After 2014 Mackevision was building up a VFX department. Alongside the movie/ TV Series jobs, they did a lot of high-quality commercial videos for clients like Mercedes and Porsche, where I was working as a Onset Supervisor around the world. At the same time I was also working for our new Future-Technology division in fields like, realtime rendering, VR and 3D scanning

3. What is your educational background?

    Rouven: I studied Communication Design at the University of Art and Design Saarbrücken (HBK Saar) with a degree as a Dipl. Designer.

4. How would you describe your current position? Most common tasks, main responsibilities and main challenges

    Rouven: I'm having a really varied position and that's one of the greatest things on it. To put it simply, the main task as a Onset Supervisor is to ensure that everything is done in a way that the effects work can later be done on time and budget. This requires close coordination with the director, camera and production during and before filming. A film/series shooting is always a very dynamic environment with a lot of spontaneous changings in schedule and requests. To handle this, you need to be very flexible and make potentially costly (or better: cost saving!) decisions within minutes.

In the area of virtual production, there are also the different technology things that you have to deal with. Often new setups and workflows have to be developed for these projects that have not been done before by us or in general. It is important to always be up to date with the latest technology in order to provide the best possible solution to the customer. Such a solution always needs to be balanced between visual fidelity and cost effectiveness.

Due to my very broadly diversified experience and my skills as a trouble shooter, I am often consulted by other departments within Accenture on technology.

5. Are you happy at your current position or are you aiming for a different role?

Rouven: I love my job and the trust that is placed in me. No reason to look for another role.

6. What advice would you give to a student or a junior artist aiming for your job?

Rouven: You have to be very interested in learning new things at all times. Flexibility, spontaneity and the joy of solving problems are the keys to success. If you think that a film set is a glamorous working environment, then I'm sorry to disappoint you.

Stephan Schäfholz—VFX Supervisor

1. What is your current position and how long have you had the job?

Stephan: I currently work as a VFX Supervisor at Accenture Song, a role I've held since 2021. I've been with the company (formerly known as Mackevision) since 2016.

2. What was your career path to get to your current position? How did you start and what other positions did you have along the way?

Stephan: My career has been a dynamic journey across multiple disciplines, countries, and prestigious companies. I started as a 3D generalist, lighting artist, and motion graphics artist at smaller studios. These early roles allowed me to explore various aspects of the visual effects pipeline. Because these projects were typically small, I often handled multiple tasks, which gave me a holistic understanding of the production process. As I gained experience, I discovered my passion for compositing—the final step where everything comes together to create a cohesive, magical image. The satisfaction of crafting the final look and bringing a shot to life drew me deeper into this specialization.

In 2009, I joined Pixomondo as a compositor, working on major projects like Hugo Cabret, Red Tails, Fast Five, Sucker Punch, The Ghostwriter, and Star Trek Into

Darkness. These projects laid the groundwork for my expertise in compositing. My move to Industrial Light & Magic (ILM) in 2012 marked a turning point, where I worked on Marvel's The Avengers under VFX Supervisor Jeff White. This was a transformative experience that deepened my technical skills and understanding of large-scale VFX production. After a stint in London at Pixomondo, I transitioned to Framestore as a Lead Compositor, contributing to Jupiter Ascending. Shortly after, I returned to ILM San Francisco in 2014 to work on Unbroken with Bill George and Agent Carter with Richard Bluff, followed by Jurassic World with Tim Alexander. These experiences significantly shaped my approach to VFX.

In 2015, I moved back to London to work at ILM on Spectre with Mark Bakowski, a supervisor I had previously collaborated with on Jupiter Ascending. Each project and supervisor had a profound influence on my growth and working style.

Wanting to return to Germany for family reasons, I joined Mackevision (now Accenture Song) in 2015 as a Senior Compositor. During this time, I worked on Game of Thrones (Seasons 6 and 7), which were remarkable due to their visual complexity. In 2017, I advanced to Compositing Supervisor and led teams on Lost in Space (Seasons 1 and 2). This role involved technical look development, problem-solving, and managing a talented team of artists. I also contributed to the historical film The Captain (2017), which required a blend of emotional storytelling and technical finesse.

Today, as a VFX Supervisor, I guide the development of visual effects on diverse projects, blending my technical expertise and creative vision. Every step of my journey has led me here, and I continue to find immense joy in creating and collaborating.

3. What is your educational background?
    Stephan: I hold a diploma in Media Engineering from the Hochschule der Medien in Stuttgart.

The degree is not specifically aimed at VFX, but rather a broad deep dive into a lot of aspects of media production. I learned a lot about photography, audio production, IT, interactive Media, shooting on film and many other things.

I find this wide range of knowledge quite helpful nowadays since the problems we deal with in VFX are quite complex and often involve a lot of different departments and technologies that you need to combine in the end.

4. How would you describe your current position? Most common tasks, main responsibilities and main challenges
    Stephan: My primary role as a VFX Supervisor is to translate the client's vision into actionable tasks that ultimately result in visually compelling images. This involves breaking down the project into manageable pieces and ensuring that all these elements integrate seamlessly in the final product.

On a daily basis, I work closely with department supervisors to tackle technical and creative challenges. Problem-solving is a significant part of the job, often involving creative interpretation to determine how specific visuals should look. Some common challenges include:

- Shot Scheduling: Ensuring tasks are completed on time.
- Technical Approaches: Finding the best methods to achieve the desired effects.
- Team Management: Assigning the right people to the right tasks.
- Software/Hardware Solutions: Making sure the tools and technology are in place.
- Pipeline Development: Building or refining workflows to optimize efficiency.

Above all, having a clear reference or concept to work toward is crucial for aligning the team's efforts and achieving the desired visual outcome.

5. Are you happy at your current position or are you aiming for a different role?

Stephan: Very happy in my current role and enjoying every project so far.

6. What advice would you give to a student or a junior artist aiming for your job?

Stephan: There are a couple of things that I learned from other people over the years that can be put in catchy phrases.

Here are some of them, which usually start to make sense after a couple of years.

It's a marathon not a sprint!

Stay curious!

It's a people business!

Robert Freitag—Freelancer

Born in February of 1986

1. What is your current position and how long have you had the job?

Robert: I currently work as a freelancer and have been doing so since 2006—almost hitting the 20-year mark.

2. What was your career path to get to your current position? How did you start and what other positions did you have along the way?

Robert: It's kind of a long story, but I'll keep it short.

FIGURE 12.4 Photo of Robert with one of his chickens.

When I was in middle school, my friend Peter told me about his brother Willi, who worked as a 3D artist for a major film company.

This was around 2003. Peter mentioned that Willi was entirely self-taught—he had made it into the industry without a university degree or any formal education. He just got his hands on a piece of software called 3D Studio Max, started doing tutorials, and simply kept improving over time.

I was instantly intrigued. At that time, I had no idea what I wanted to do with my life, but 3D computer graphics had already fascinated me—especially the cinematics for pc games.

I asked Peter for a copy of 3Ds Max, and he was kind enough to burn it onto a CD for me. That day quite literally changed my life. 3D graphics became not just my biggest hobby, but a passion unlike anything I had ever experienced.

The artistic freedom to create anything—from spaceships and cities to characters, star systems, and strange new worlds—was mind-blowing, and it still is today.

At the time, social media didn't really exist, so online forums were the best places to learn and share ideas. I spent hours every day on 3Dmax.de and CGTalk.com. Over time, I made online friends who were just as new to 3D as I was. I still remember the endless Skype group calls we had after school, often going late into the night—trying out new techniques, challenging ourselves to become better both technically and artistically.

When I finished middle school, I casually mentioned it in a forum post. Not long after, I received an email from a guy named Michael, who had been following my journey for some time. He offered me a traineeship at his company Ground Studios in Düsseldorf. It was a dream come true, and I happily accepted my first job in the industry.

Ground Studios was made up of talented generalists who worked across various industries—games, VFX, animation, architectural visualization, and game cinematics. Michael, Peter, and Martin were fantastic, and I learned a lot during my time there.

Among the software they used were 3Ds Max and a renderer called finalRender by cebas Visual Technology. Michael, my boss, was a big fan of finalRender and even served as a beta tester. Since many of my tasks involved rendering, he arranged for me to join the beta program as well. This allowed me to report bugs, suggest features, and eventually meet cebas' CEO, Edwin Braun, who later became a good friend as well.

Over the next 2 years, I became the top poster on the beta forums for finalRender and thinkingParticles, getting heavily involved with the developers and even contributing some code.

In 2008, Edwin told me about a movie project: 2012, directed by Roland Emmerich.

He explained that a company called Uncharted Territory was using final-Render on the film and needed specialists to help with technical challenges. He asked if I would be interested. I was 21 at the time, and the job would mean moving to Los Angeles for at least a year.

It was the opportunity of a lifetime—I accepted immediately, moved out of my parents' house, and into my first LA apartment.

Working on my first Hollywood movie was incredible.

Uncharted Territory, led by Volker Engel and Marc Weigert, operated like a "pop-up" company—assembling teams of freelancers and infrastructure on-the-fly for each Roland Emmerich film.

The 2012 VFX team was based on the Sony lot in Culver City. My official title was Lighting TD (Technical Director). My primary responsibility was handling rendering challenges and assembling complex scenes, though I also contributed to FX work thanks to my experience with thinkingParticles.

The camaraderie and sheer talent gathered from all over the world at Uncharted made it a truly special place to work. The friendships, the energy, and the sense of shared adventure were unforgettable, and I'm incredibly grateful to have been a part of it. After 2012, I continued freelancing in the US for a few more years before returning to Germany. Since then, I have freelanced for multiple VFX companies across Germany, Canada, and the United States—mainly focusing on lighting, rendering, and FX work.

3. What is your educational background?
   Robert: My formal educational background is quite minimal—
   I only have a middle school diploma.
4. How would you describe your current position? Most common
   tasks, main responsibilities and main challenges
   Robert: Currently, I work as a classic freelancer.

I have an established network of friends and recurring clients in the industry, and I work on a variety of projects, mainly related to VFX shot production. Occasionally, I also do on-set supervision.

In recent years, I have expanded my activities:

I started a side business assembling CG workstations and server infrastructures tailored for film production companies.

I also set up a render farm on a major cloud infrastructure provider, which I rent out or customize for studios and individuals in need of powerful, temporary rendering solutions.

5. Are you happy at your current position or are you aiming for a different role?
   Robert: Absolutely—I couldn't be happier!
6. What advice would you give to a student or a junior artist aiming for your job?
   Robert: Practice mindfulness.

Reading all these interviews it should become very clear that there's no single route to success in the VFX world. Artists enter the industry through different doors and advance at different paces. Among many valuable lessons you can take from these interviews,

LESSONS FROM ACCOMPLISHED VFX PROFESSIONALS

Across the industry, experienced professionals consistently echo a few key lessons—hard-earned truths about growth, collaboration, and creativity under pressure. Some of these were coincidentally expressed in the interviews in the previous chapter.

A. **Learn to Communicate, Not Just Create**
   • Artistic skill opens doors, but communication skills help you walk through them.

- Whether giving feedback, asking for help, or presenting work to clients, clear, thoughtful communication often determines how far you advance.

B. **Feedback is a Gift**
- Learning to accept critique without defensiveness is a critical professional skill.
- The best artists seek feedback early and often, using it as a tool to sharpen their craft—not as a judgment of their worth.

C. **Specialize, Then Broaden (or Vice Versa)**
- Some careers flourish by diving deep into one area; others evolve by bouncing between disciplines.
- Regardless of strategy, the artists who thrive are those who remain curious, adaptable, and open to shifting goals.

D. **Trust the Long Game**
- Progress in VFX is rarely linear. Some years bring rapid growth; others feel stagnant.
- Building a sustainable career means pacing yourself, staying connected to your creative drive, and being okay with temporary setbacks.

COPING WITH INDUSTRY FLUCTUATIONS AND JOB INSECURITY

The VFX industry is known for its volatility. Projects come and go, studios expand and contract, and artists often face layoffs, relocations, or dry spells between gigs. In this chapter, we explore how professionals manage the uncertainties and maintain stability amid an unstable landscape.

A. **Embracing the Freelance Mindset**
- Even staff artists benefit from thinking like freelancers: tracking finances, building a professional network, and staying portfolio-ready at all times.
- Freelancers, in turn, thrive when they treat their work like a business—managing rates, client relationships, and time with purpose.

B. **Preparing for Transitions**
- Keeping your demo reel updated, nurturing relationships with former colleagues, and maintaining visibility on platforms

FIGURE 12.5 Personal project of character development from a cool concept I found

like ArtStation or LinkedIn helps you stay employable during gaps.
- Emotional preparation matters too. Understanding that layoffs and project endings are common—not personal—can ease the mental toll.

C. **Building Financial Resilience**
  - Saving during busy seasons, budgeting for down periods, and avoiding lifestyle inflation are essential strategies.
  - Some artists create side income through tutorials, asset sales, or part-time teaching to smooth out income variability.
D. **Staying Grounded During Uncertainty**
  - Finding support in community—online groups, friends in the industry, or even peer mentorship—can help navigate tough moments.
  - Mental health practices, exercise, and creative hobbies outside of work help maintain perspective.

STRATEGIES FOR WORK-LIFE BALANCE

In a high-pressure, deadline-driven field, maintaining a healthy work-life balance can feel like a luxury. But it's actually a necessity for long-term success and personal well-being. At times this may become impossible but it's important not to forget that as much as we love our work: we work so we can live, we don't live so we can work. If the imbalance persists for too long

FIGURE 12.6 Another frame capture from a personal project animation called Mood Swings

or too frequently, you should take action to restore and protect that balance. Otherwise, sooner or later, your mind and/or your body will do it for you.

A. **Setting Boundaries Without Burning Bridges**
- Saying "no" is a skill—especially when projects stretch beyond expected hours.
- Communicate clearly, plan your time, and negotiate respectfully when expectations become unrealistic.

B. **Protecting Time for Yourself**
- Whether it's family, rest, or creative exploration, make time for activities that nourish your mental and emotional health.
- Many experienced professionals carve out weekends, take scheduled breaks between contracts, or establish strict "no laptop after 7pm" rules.

C. **Remote Work and Flexibility**
- Remote workflows have opened up new ways to balance personal needs with professional responsibilities.
- Use this flexibility wisely—structure your day, create routines, and separate your workspace from your living space where possible.

D. **Defining Your Own Version of Success**
- For some, success means working on blockbuster films; for others, it's creative freedom, location independence, or time with loved ones.
- Knowing your own goals helps you make career decisions that align with your values—not just industry norms.

Final Thoughts: Learning from Real Lives

The VFX industry is built on craft, yes—but also on character. These stories and strategies reflect the deeper side of the profession: the challenges of growth, the richness of collaboration, and the personal resilience that fuels every frame of magic on screen.

Whether you're just starting or already deep in your journey, take these lessons as reminders: you're not alone, the path isn't always straight, and your story matters too.

Preparing for the Future of VFX Careers

13

The visual effects industry has always evolved hand in hand with technology. As new tools, platforms, and workflows emerge, artists must continuously adapt to stay relevant—and competitive. This section looks ahead, examining where the industry is headed and how you can position yourself for long-term success. From adapting to real-time pipelines and virtual production to building a future-proof skillset, this is about more than just staying current—it's about staying valuable.

EMBRACING EMERGING TECHNOLOGIES AND NEW WORKFLOWS

In recent years, we've seen paradigm shifts in how VFX is produced. New workflows are streamlining processes, and emerging technologies are changing the very definition of visual effects work. If you're just starting out or aiming to grow your career, keeping pace with these changes is no longer optional.

- **Real-Time Rendering and Virtual Production**
  - Tools like **Unreal Engine** and **Unity** are becoming integral to VFX pipelines—no longer just for previsualization, but for final-quality output.
  - Virtual production using LED volumes and real-time environments is transforming how sets are built and filmed.
  - Artists familiar with real-time engines, scene optimization, and scripting will have a significant edge.
- **AI and Machine Learning in VFX**
  - AI is increasingly used in areas like **roto, cleanup, tracking, simulation**, and **denoising**.

DOI: 10.1201/9781003494485-13

- Instead of replacing artists, these tools often **augment productivity**, automating repetitive tasks so you can focus on creative problem-solving.
- Learning how to **work with AI**—and when not to—will be a critical skill for tomorrow's professionals.
- **Procedural and Non-Destructive Workflows**
  - Software like **Houdini, Substance Designer**, and **Katana** promote scalable, procedural setups that can handle complex variations with fewer manual adjustments.
  - Studios favor artists who can build smart, reusable systems that make large-scale projects more efficient.
- **Cross-Disciplinary Integration**
  - VFX is converging with games, XR, advertising, and even architecture and product design.
  - Skills in real-time interactivity, technical art, and multi-platform deployment are opening doors far beyond traditional film and TV.
- **Cloud-Based Collaboration**
  - Remote work is here to stay. Studios increasingly rely on cloud infrastructure for **storage, rendering**, and **review workflows**.
  - Familiarity with platforms like **ShotGrid, SyncSketch**, and **AWS-based pipelines** will become standard.

BUILDING A FUTURE-PROOF VFX CAREER

How do you prepare for a future that's constantly shifting? The key lies in adaptability, curiosity, and a clear understanding of your goals. This chapter focuses on strategies that can help you thrive over the long term—through industry changes, economic shifts, or personal reinvention.

A. **Adopt a Growth Mindset**
   - The most successful artists view their careers as **ongoing experiments**.
   - Accept that discomfort and uncertainty are part of growth. Embrace change as an opportunity, not a threat.
B. **Balance Breadth with Depth**
   - **T-shaped professionals**—those with deep expertise in one area and a working knowledge of adjacent fields—are particularly valuable.
   - Specialize where it suits your strengths but stay flexible and willing to learn across disciplines.

C. **Keep Your Portfolio and Knowledge Current**
  - Update your reel and resume **at least annually**, even when you're not job-hunting.
  - Follow updates from key software providers, read white papers, and explore new tools during downtime between projects.

D. **Invest in Transferable Skills**
  - **Problem-solving, communication, feedback processing**, and **leadership** are timeless skills that transcend software and workflow changes.
  - They also help you **move laterally**—from artist to lead, to supervisor, or even to different industries that value visual storytelling.

E. **Diversify Your Opportunities**
  - Don't rely solely on employment. Many VFX artists explore **teaching, consulting, tool development**, or **asset sales** as complementary income streams.
  - Others pivot into adjacent careers like **virtual production, game development**, or **technical direction**.

F. **Build a Resilient Network**
  - Your network is your career safety net. Stay in touch with colleagues, attend events (virtually or in person), and help others when you can.
  - When layoffs or transitions come—and they often do—it's your relationships that will help you bounce back fastest.

Final Thoughts: Preparing for the Unknown

No one can predict exactly what VFX will look like in 5 or 10 years. But those who stay curious, flexible, and proactive will continue to find a place in it. The future favors those who prepare—not with fear, but with intention. By embracing change and investing in your growth, you're not just surviving in this industry—you're shaping it.

Conclusion 14

The journey through a VFX career isn't a straight line—it's a layered, looping, and evolving path. Whether you're just starting out or looking back on years of experience, the field continues to challenge, reward, and transform those who commit to it. This final section offers a moment to zoom out and reflect on what this book has aimed to provide: clarity, confidence, and a sense of community for every kind of VFX professional.

WHAT I WISH I KNEW STARTING OUT

Looking back, there are several things I wish someone had told me when I first stepped into the world of CG and VFX. Maybe they did and I wasn't listening, or maybe I just wasn't ready to hear it. If I could speak to that younger version of myself—and to anyone starting out today—here's what I'd say:

- **Your path doesn't need to be perfect—it needs to be yours.** You don't need to know everything up front. You'll learn by doing, and your direction will evolve.
- **Mastery takes time.** No single course, software, or job will make you "ready." Show up consistently, stay curious, and commit to progress, not perfection.
- **Soft skills will take you further than any toolset.** Learn how to take feedback, communicate clearly, and collaborate respectfully. These are what make you someone others want to work with.
- **You'll fail sometimes. That's part of growth.** A failed render, a lost job, or a blown deadline is not the end—it's part of the real learning.
- **Don't wait to "arrive" before you start contributing.** Share your process. Ask questions. Help others. That's how you become part of the industry, not just an applicant to it.

DOI: 10.1201/9781003494485-14

ADVICE TO THE FUTURE
GENERATIONS OF VFX ARTISTS

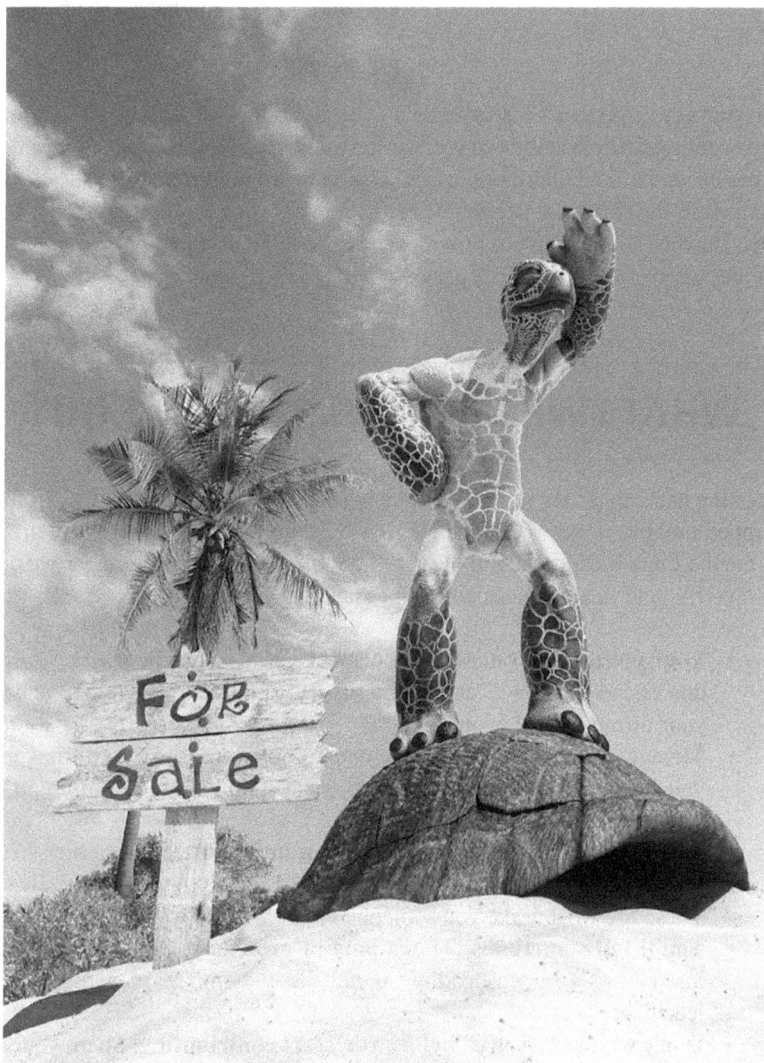

FIGURE 14.1   Turtle Freedom for Sale—another personal project from 2012.

Every artist who picks up a stylus, fires up Houdini, opens Nuke, or lights a shot in Unreal is joining a tradition that's only a few decades old—but growing at light speed. Here's what I want to pass on to those who will carry the industry into the next era:

- **Curiosity is your greatest asset.** The software will change. The workflows will change. What won't change is the need for people who want to learn.
- **Ask better questions.** Don't just ask how—ask why. Dig into the context behind the tools. Understand what problem you're solving before you solve it.
- **Value your well-being.** Burnout is not a badge of honor. Rest, relationships, and play are not luxuries—they are fuel for sustainable creativity.
- **Be generous.** Share what you learn. Teach others. Encourage peers. This is not a zero-sum game—your growth makes space for others to grow, too.
- **Create your own definition of success.** Some of you will become supervisors, other specialists, educators, or indie filmmakers. Some will stay generalists forever—and love it. All of those paths are valid.

THANK YOU AND LOOKING FORWARD

Thank you for reading this book—whether you skipped around, read it cover to cover, or used it as a reference as you found your way. I wrote it because I needed a book like this when I was finding mine.

To every artist who gave their time, insight, and personal stories—thank you. This book exists because of you. Your honesty and generosity turn information into inspiration.

To those of you just starting out: welcome. You're stepping into a world full of possibility.

To those with years of experience: thank you for helping shape the craft, the culture, and the community.

And to everyone: keep learning, keep creating, and keep supporting each other.

This is your career. This is your story. Make it beautiful.

Appendices

A. VFX ARTIST PORTFOLIO DEVELOPMENT CHECKLIST

✓ Core Components

- **Desmo Reel (60–90 Seconds)**
  - Focused, concise, and well-edited
  - Strongest work at the beginning
  - Clean, readable title card with your name, role, and contact info
  - Label your role in each shot (e.g., "FX only," "Lighting + Comp")
  - Only include work you understand deeply and can discuss
- **Project Breakdowns**
  - Written breakdown for each reel shot (text or PDF)
  - Explain your responsibilities, tools used, challenges solved
  - Optional: add a video breakdown (before/after, wireframes, passes)
- **Still Portfolio (Optional)**
  - High-resolution stills of your best work
  - Especially useful for modelers, texture/surfacing artists, matte painters
  - Organize into categories: characters, environments, FX, etc.

⚒ Technical Content (Pick Based on Your Specialty)

For FX Artists

- Simulations (fire, smoke, destruction, water)
- Particle systems (rain, debris, magical effects)
- Procedural setups (with variations)
- Emphasize realism, scale, and control

For Compositors

- Multi-pass integration of CG and live action
- Green screen keying, clean-up, matchmoving
- Color grading and lighting continuity
- Before/after comparisons

For Modelers/Surfacing Artists

- Clean topology and UVs
- Sculpted detail (ZBrush, Mudbox, etc.)
- Texturing with maps (diffuse, roughness, normal, etc.)
- Turntables and wireframe views

For Animators

- Body mechanics (walks, runs, jumps)
- Acting shots with strong emotion
- Creature animation (weight, realism)
- Use rigs legally allowed in reels (no commercial IP misuse)

🌐 Online Presence

- **ArtStation or portfolio website** (clean and up to date)
- **Vimeo or YouTube channel** with your reel
- Resume (PDF, 1-page) with relevant skills and experience
- LinkedIn profile reflecting your current goals and projects
- Use consistent naming, branding, and contact info

✏️ Presentation and Strategy

- Tailor your reel to your desired role (e.g., FX vs. comp)
- Don't include weak or outdated work
- Use a simple, non-distracting music track or no music at all
- Test playback on different devices for quality and legibility
- Get feedback from industry peers or mentors before finalizing

🔄 Maintenance and Growth

- Update your reel regularly (every 6–12 months or after each project)
- Keep learning new tools and adding relevant work
- Save work-in-progress breakdowns as you go—don't wait until the end
- Track which shots get the best responses for future targeting
- Have a shorter cut-down reel for specific job applications (30–45 seconds)

B. GLOSSARY OF VFX TERMINOLOGY

A

- **lpha Channel**: A grayscale channel in an image or video that defines transparency.
- **Ambient Occlusion (AO)**: A shading method that simulates soft shadows in crevices and where surfaces meet.
- **Anamorphic**: A widescreen format that horizontally compresses footage for cinematic projection.
- **Animation**: The process of creating motion by sequencing images, models, or digital objects.

B

- **Backplate**: A background image or footage onto which CG elements are composited.
- **Bezier Curve**: A mathematical curve used in animation and modeling for smooth transitions.

- **Bump Map**: A texture that simulates surface detail without changing geometry.

C

- **Camera Tracking**: Analyzing live-action footage to extract camera movement for integrating CG.
- **Compositing**: Combining multiple visual elements into a single cohesive image.
- **Color Grading**: Adjusting colors for mood, tone, and continuity.
- **Clean Plate**: A version of a shot with objects or actors removed for FX or clean-up.

D

- **Depth Map**: A grayscale image representing the distance of objects from the camera.
- **Digital Double**: A 3D model of an actor used for stunts or simulations.
- **Displacement Map**: Alters geometry based on texture information to add detail.

E

- **Environment**: Digital scenery or backgrounds in a VFX shot.
- **Edge Blend**: Softening the transition between elements to blend seamlessly.
- **Export**: Saving data in a format compatible with other software or platforms.

F

- **Frame Rate**: Number of images shown per second in animation or video (e.g., 24 fps).
- **Focal Length**: Determines the zoom and perspective of a camera lens.
- **FX (Effects)**: Simulations like fire, smoke, water, or destruction created in software.

G

- **Green Screen**: A filming technique using a green backdrop for compositing.
- **Gizmo**: A tool or script in compositing used to automate or organize tasks.
- **Global Illumination**: Lighting calculation that simulates indirect light in a scene.

H

- **HDRI (High Dynamic Range Imaging)**: Captures a wide range of light intensities for realistic lighting.
- **Hair System**: A rig or simulation for animating hair or fur.
- **Holdout**: A matte used to preserve transparency or occlusion during compositing.

I

- **In-Camera VFX**: Practical effects or virtual production captured directly on set.
- **Interpolation**: The method of generating in-between frames or key values in animation.
- **Image Plane**: A background image used as a reference in 3D space.

J

- **Jitter**: Unwanted motion or noise in animation, simulation, or rendering.

K

- **Keyframe**: A defined frame that marks the start or end of a transformation.
- **Keying**: The process of isolating a subject from a background, usually green or blue screen.

L

- **Layer**: Individual visual elements stacked in compositing or editing.

- **Look Development**: Process of defining the final appearance of assets.
- **LOD (Level of Detail)**: Reducing detail of assets based on their screen size or distance.

M

- **Matte Painting**: A painted or digitally created environment or backdrop.
- **Motion Blur**: The blur effect that simulates fast motion between frames.
- **MoCap (Motion Capture)**: Recording real-world movement for digital animation.

N

- **Node**: A functional unit in a visual graph that performs a specific operation.
- **Normals**: Vectors perpendicular to surfaces used for lighting and shading calculations.
- **NURBS**: A mathematical model for generating smooth curves and surfaces.

O

- **Occlusion**: Blocking of one object by another in 3D space.
- **Object Tracking**: Tracking the motion of a non-camera object in footage.
- **On-Set Supervision**: Ensuring proper VFX data collection during filming.

P

- **Parallax**: Perceived shift of objects due to camera movement.
- **Particle System**: Simulates effects like dust, smoke, or sparks using small elements.
- **Passes**: Rendered layers separated for compositing (e.g., shadow pass, diffuse pass).

Q

- **Quaternion**: A method for smooth rotational interpolation without gimbal lock.

R

- **Render**: The process of generating a final image or sequence from a 3D scene.
- **Rigging**: Creating a skeletal system for animating characters or objects.
- **Rotoscoping**: Manually creating mattes by tracing over footage.

S

- **Shader**: A script that defines how surfaces respond to light.
- **Specular**: The bright highlight that simulates reflection on shiny surfaces.
- **Simulation**: Physically based generation of effects like cloth, fluids, or fire.

T

- **Texture Map**: An image applied to a model's surface for detail or color.
- **Tracking Markers**: Visual references used during filming to aid matchmoving.
- **Tiling**: Repeating a texture across a surface to cover large areas.

U

- **UV Mapping**: The process of projecting a 2D image onto a 3D model.
- **Unreal Engine**: A real-time 3D engine used increasingly in VFX production.
- **Upscaling**: Increasing the resolution of footage or renders.

V

- **Vector Blur**: Motion blur effect using motion vectors between frames.
- **Virtual Camera**: A simulated camera in 3D software.
- **Volumetrics**: Simulating effects like fog, smoke, or light rays in 3D space.

W

- **Wireframe**: A skeletal view of 3D geometry shosswing edges and vertices.
- **Workflow**: The organized sequence of tasks in a production pipeline.
- **World Space**: The global coordinate system of a 3D scene.

X

- **XGen**: A grooming system in Maya used for hair, fur, and instancing.

Y

- **Y-Axis**: In most 3D systems, the vertical axis in a coordinate space.

Z

- **Z-Depth**: Data that represents distance from the camera for depth-based effects.
- **ZBrush**: A sculpting program widely used for high-resolution modeling.

For Product Safety Concerns and Information please contact our EU
representative GPSR@taylorandfrancis.com
Taylor & Francis Verlag GmbH, Kaufingerstraße 24, 80331 München, Germany

www.ingramcontent.com/pod-product-compliance
Lightning Source LLC
Chambersburg PA
CBHW070737220326
41598CB00024BA/3458